FIERCE

OUR TESTIMONIES ARE *FIERCE*
AND MEANT TO BE SHARED

One *FIERCE* Lady

TRILOGY CHRISTIAN PUBLISHERS
TUSTIN, CA

Trilogy Christian Publishers
A Wholly Owned Subsidiary of Trinity Broadcasting Network
2442 Michelle Drive
Tustin, CA 92780

10 9 8 7 6 5 4 3 2 1

Library of Congress Cataloging-in-Publication Data is available.
ISBN 978-1-64773-442-8
ISBN 978-1-64773-443-5 (ebook)

Contents

Dedications

I would like to dedicate this book to my children, my grandchildren, and my generations to come. I pray that your faith sustains you and may you know that I have left for you a legacy of faith. I have continued to pray for you all. Even if you did not want me to. I love you all more than you could ever know.

I also dedicate this book to anyone who is feeling like they are broken and alone. May you feel His love and be strengthened along this journey of life by the Word of God and by your personal relationship with Christ Jesus.

Thank you for taking the time to read this book of healing through shared testimonies. May you be inspired to embrace His healing presence in all of life's storms.

Foreword

Lisa has been a tremendous sister in the kingdom to me. I have known her for over ten years and her genuine, authentic passion for God and for others grows like a palm tree. She demonstrates true servanthood in her desire to just be there whenever there is a need. This book is not only one of the greatest books I have read, but it is her real, raw life experiences of how God manifested His power, love, greatness, protection, healing, and presence through every victorious battle. I hope you get the chance to not only read with blessed eyes but, hear with blessed ears the reenactment when she narrates her story.

One day sitting in my home, she opens this binder that I thought was her jewelry collection. As she humbly asks if it is alright to read, and turns the leaves of each page, I could hear, I could feel, I journeyed with her through the valley of the shadow of death in my own experiences. And for the first time knowing that this anointed woman had been through a few things, but without fear, unafraid, unashamed because the Lord God Almighty was always there (*let God arise and let His enemies be scattered*) and showed Himself strong and covenant-keeping.

Congratulations and thank you, Lisa, for sharing this book with me while it was still in your womb. My first opinion was what an excellent women's ministry tool...no, I was wrong, this testimony, this treasure, this wonderful writing will minister to every creed. My prayer is for this book to reach and be published in many nations. May every reader understand and realize that in our "flagship moments" (the peaks, the pits, and the transitions), we focus not on the battle, but the results.

Apostle Paul says,

> *What then [does it matter]? So long as in every way, whether in pretense [for self-promotion] or in all honesty [to spread the truth], Christ is being preached; and in this I rejoice.*
>
> *Yes, and I will rejoice [later as well], for I know [with confidence] that this will turn out for my deliverance and spiritual well-being, through your prayers and the [superabundant] supply of the Spirit of Jesus Christ [which upholds me]. It is my own eager expectation and hope, that [looking toward the future] I will not disgrace myself nor be ashamed in anything, but that with courage and the utmost freedom of speech, even now as always,*

Christ will be magnified and exalted in my body,
whether by life or by death.

Philippians 1:18-20 (AMP)

In closing, I am reminded of the passage in Psalm
23:5-6 (AMP),

You prepare a table before me in the presence of
my enemies. You have anointed and refreshed my
head with oil; My cup overflows. Surely goodness
and mercy and unfailing love shall follow me
all the days of my life, And I shall dwell forever
[throughout all my days] in the house and in the
presence of the Lord.

Fear, oppression, depression, sickness and disease,
suicide, addiction, domestic- violence, sexual assault,
self-harm, low self-esteem, and church hurt no longer
have a hold on us.

~ Cheryl Hawkins
Minister of Music

A Letter From Pastors

As Sr. Pastors and spiritual parents to many, our spirits are always lifted when we hear our children walk in truth. Lisa Adams is an individual that exemplifies that statement. From the time that Lisa and her family connected with Gwen and I, and the ministries of Church Without Walls in Harrisburg, Pennsylvania, her faithfulness and loyalty to the "Kingdom of God," our church and other relationships have been unswerving.

Through the years, we have had the privilege of watching her grow as a woman, mother, and spiritual daughter. We are honored to say, you will not find a more loving, caring, and compassionate soul on this planet. We have witnessed firsthand and are proud that she has become a doer of the Word and not a forgetful hearer. She has learned to use her faith purposefully and is now seen as one who possesses victorious, overcoming faith.

Because of her deep appreciation and thankfulness to God for His forgiveness, mercy, and healing in her own life, Lisa is driven to reach everyone she can with the message of hope. She has a relentless drive to "do unto others" and help those who are many times forgotten, overlooked, or neglected. Her own experience with God has helped her personally understand the power of relationship and to become established in the righteousness that only comes through faith in Jesus Christ.

As Lisa looked for ways to expand her ministry, sphere of influence, and to reach more people with the love of God and the message, "You are not alone," she was inspired to write this book of short stories and testimonies. These divine testimonies of inner healing, physical healing, and delivering power are taken from the script of her life. The script, though finished before the foundations of the world, is still being written as Lisa continues her journey and encounters more and more people, just like you.

The challenges, disappointments, dreams dashed, and testimonies of dreams fulfilled are all met via the vehicle of a life lived and faith expressed. The following collection of stories taken from a few of Lisa's life experiences are sure to minister life, hope, healing, joy, and even overcoming faith.

We are immensely proud of Lisa as she walks by faith and daily resumes her pursuit of God. I often say, "A man with a testimony is never at the mercy of a man with an argument." Maybe some of these snippets taken from real-life experiences will help you gain the upper hand in one of your life's arguments.

Maybe, just maybe this will be the way you encounter Lisa, her faith, and her God. It is our prayer that one or more of these testimonies will begin, add to, or complete a work in you, resulting in your very own testimony of overcoming faith and healing.

Enjoy!

Philip and Gwen Thornton
Sr. Pastors of Legacy Faith Church
104 Roberts Valley Rd.
Harrisburg, PA 17110

Acknowledgements

Father God, "thank you" does not quite hit the mark with what you have done for me. It just does not seem adequate to express the gratitude in which I have for You or the sacrifice that You have made on my behalf through Your Son, Jesus Christ. However, I thank You and come to You with a grateful heart.

Rejoice in the Lord always [delight, take pleasure in Him]; again, I will say, rejoice! Let your gentle spirit [your graciousness, unselfishness, mercy, tolerance, and patience] be known to all people. The Lord is near. Do not be anxious or worried about anything, but in everything [every circumstance and situation] by prayer and petition with thanksgiving, continue to make your [specific] requests known to God. And the peace of God [that peace which reassures the heart, that peace] which transcends all understanding, [that peace which]

stands guard over your hearts and your minds in
Christ Jesus [is yours].

Philippians 4:4-7 (AMP)

To my husband Ray, for supporting the vision of this book and understanding the call on our lives. Thank you for encouraging me even when life's storms were swirling around us.

Thank you to all the ladies who have shared their journey of healing openly in this book with the hope that others will receive healing and draw closer to God once again.

Thank you to my spiritual parents, Apostle Dr. Philip Thornton, and Pastor Gwen Thornton, for taking the time to teach and equip me with the Word of God and especially for not sugar-coating it. "Facts are subject to change but, truth is eternal." ~ Apostle Dr. Thornton.

Thank you to my children and grandchildren for just being you. God has a plan and a purpose for each of you.

Thank you to my sweet friend Carol for sowing her time and gifts to type this book amidst all the different "hats" she wears. You totally rock.

Thank you to my dear sweet friend, Elaine Bish of White Deer Photography, for your willingness, ability, and your gifting. You are an amazing photographer may your photography business continuously prosper.

Thank you to my fellow Wordsmiths group for your encouragement and prayers.

Thank you to everyone who sowed a financial seed into this project.

Thank you most of all for your prayers and encouragement. I love and appreciate you all.

Introduction

Congratulations! By picking up this book you are joining some amazing women on a journey of revealing and healing.

The topics shared in this book will touch your heart and prayerfully expose and heal some areas you thought were too painful to deal with.

Beginning with who these women are, what happened in their lives—despair, violence, illness, death, marriage, pain, healing, spiritual awakening— and the strength to get up and move on to live healthy lives.

How, with the power of forgiveness and with all that has happened in their lives, they are willing to share so others who are still battling can find the strength, encouragement, and inspiration to begin their own journey knowing they are not alone, and this is why the book is needed.

I will come with the mighty acts of the Lord God [and in His strength]; I will make mention of Your righteousness, Yours alone.

Psalm 71:16 (AMP)

Disclaimer

It is my belief that everyone should read this book. Perhaps you have never faced any of the circumstances that are shared in the pages that follow. So then why? Simply because at some point in your life if it has not happened to you, it may have happened to someone you know and/or care about. This book is not meant as a gossiping tool; this book is to reveal, to inspire, and to help heal.

By reading this book that openly discusses personal battles and triumphs I pray that any storm, heartache, or tragedy that you may have encountered in your personal life be healed. Please be aware that many personal abuse situations are openly shared, so if you do not feel comfortable continuing to read on, I pray that you at least understand the importance of the overcomers' testimony and how we have found healing in Christ Jesus.

I pray that you read this book with an open heart. I pray that you are encouraged and allow the Holy Spirit to heal areas in your heart you have hidden away or even areas that you feel have power over you.

O my love, you are altogether beautiful and fair. There is no flaw nor blemish in you!

Song of Solomon 4:7 (AMP)

The names in this book have been changed to protect the innocent.

I chose the Amplified version of the Bible to give more detail to the reader.

Why FIERCE?

Fierce: Having or displaying an intense or ferocious aggressiveness.

This definition is taken from the Oxford dictionary.

To be *Fierce* in one's testimony is a good thing.

Bottom Line: Aggressiveness is what is required by peacemakers not peacekeepers and that takes a fierceness. What good is a FIERCE testimony if we do not share it?

Our testimonies are FIERCE and meant to be shared.

Blessed [spiritually calm with life-joy in God's favor] are the makers and maintainers of peace, for they will [express His character and] be called the sons of God.

Matthew 5:9 (AMP)

It takes one to know one.

"When a woman is strong in spirit, she knows she can accomplish whatever it takes to rise above her circumstances."

~ *Lisa A., One FIERCE Lady*

Poem

I may look strong,
I may act tough,
But the woman who stands before you has had enough.
Your words can cut, and your violence can bruise,
But the woman who stands before you is tired of being
used.
I stand here proud to speak out loud against the hurt,
Because my spirit has been strengthened by the God I
serve.
You thought I would not rise again,
You were wrong.
You thought I would not answer the call on my life,
You were wrong.
Not by my strength,
Yet by my Faith,
My God has made me strong.

~ Lisa A., One FIERCE Lady

The Purpose of This Book

The purpose of this book is that it is meant to inspire, reveal, and heal.

To encourage individuals from all walks of life that you are not alone, and that the book is to be used as a tool to help in the healing process.

To expose those ugly things that try to hinder us from complete forgiveness, healing, and wholeness.

If only one person should receive healing from the shared life experiences in this book, then Praise God because you are worthy.

This reminds me of the parable of the lost sheep,

What do you think? If a man has a hundred sheep, and one of them gets lost, will he not leave the ninety-nine on the mountain and go in search of the one that is lost?

Matthew 18:12 (AMP)

He loves all of us this much, so much that what the enemy planned for evil, God has turned around for good.

Like the story of Joseph in the book of Genesis. Joseph was sold into slavery by his own brothers and is now prosperous and able to forgive and be a blessing during a great famine to the very individuals that sold him into slavery.

As for you, you meant evil against me, but God meant it for good in order to bring about this present outcome, that many people would be kept alive [as they are this day].

Genesis 50:20 (AMP)

Have you ever heard someone say, "Anything hidden in darkness has power over you?" I have heard it many times and at first, I thought it was some form of "Christian-ease." It is not, as His children and joint-heirs with Christ Jesus, we are the light of this world because Christ is in us.

You are the light of [Christ to] the world. A city set on a hill cannot be hidden.

Matthew 5:14 (AMP)

The enemy knows we are the light of Christ in this world and will TRY to hinder the light with his own darkness.

This little light of mine, I am going to let it shine. (Singing)

So, as you read the following testimonies of some amazing women who share openly, be inspired to give to God whatever you thought might be too depressing, horrible, or ugly and embrace a liberating life experience that will change you forever.

Remember Jesus loves you and so do I.

Thirst

When my sister in Christ shared with me what the Holy Spirit had given her on thirst and asked if she could share it in this book, I thought to myself, "What a perfect beginning to what this book is about!"

Do we thirst to bring others closer to Christ? Are we examples here on earth?

Jesus' thirst should be our goal, to thirst to see others set free from the prison of sin, pain, and anguish.

To let everyone see and experience the life-giving water that only Christ may quench in this arid life.

He wills that our souls be quenched with living water so that we will never be thirsty again.

In the pages of this book that follow may His Word quench your thirst and heal your soul, for Christ is the hope that you shall never thirst again.

After this, Jesus, knowing that all was now finished, said in fulfillment of the Scripture, "I am thirsty."

John 19:28 (AMP)

The book of John, Chapter 1, exposes to us that in the beginning was the Word, and the Word was with God, and the Word was God, and the Word was the light, the Word was made flesh, the Word was Jesus.

He was sent to light our way, to bring us from the dark prison of sin into the marvelous light, to bring us the freedom of salvation through grace and faith, to bring us the acceptance of Jesus into our hearts. We are saved.

He came to be our perfect example. He left his glorious home on high to take on the form of man. He suffered poverty, loneliness, scorn, temptation, thirst, grief and sorrow, shed his precious blood, and bore all our sins. He bore it all that he might have compassion upon us as we face these things. But he overcame. He rose the victor to show that we too can overcome.

In my Bible, I read that Jesus was on that cruel cross for six hours. But Jesus, being King of kings and Lord of lords, the great I am, through his agony, was still doing good works! He was seeing after others. He prayed for the rulers and soldiers saying, "Father, forgive them for they know not what they do." He assured the dying thief of salvation saying, "Today shalt thou be with me in paradise."

He looked down upon his mother and gave her over into the keeping and care of John, the beloved disciple.

Finally, realizing he had finished His work for others, His flesh took over and He said, "I thirst."

They gave Him wine mixed with gall to drink, but Matthew 27:34 (AMP) tells us after tasting it, He would not drink. My thought is that this thirst for drink typifies the reason for His priceless sacrifice. His great thirst for souls. My dictionary tells me that to thirst is a painful feeling caused by having nothing to drink. I like to think that Jesus was still thinking of others and setting a final example for us. We should have a painful feeling in our hearts caused by not having souls to lay before the master, we need a thirst for souls and to teach others to walk in sonship.

1 Timothy 4:12 (AMP) says in part, *"Set a pattern for the believers in speech, in conduct, in love, in faith, and in [moral] purity."*

Our duty as Christians is to be living examples of Christ in word, thought, and deed. We need to put our faith in action, for in every sinner is a potential saint. No Christian life is to be lived in vain. Christ presents the challenge to us to thirst for souls. We should grasp every opportunity to witness for our Lord in whatever way he leads us.

There are so many souls gone astray, so many young and old who have died in their sins. Could we have won them for Christ? Did we thirst for them to be set free?

I read an article about a career woman who was shocked by the simple statement of faith a young girl gave of her saying, "I want to be just like you when I grow up." It shocked her in the right direction. It shocked her into looking into the mirror of her life to evaluate if she was letting Christ's spirit control her and shine through her. She told how in the years since, when faced with decisions, this girl comes to mind and she is careful to see that Christ is directing.

Jesus said in John 9:4, *"We must work the works of Him who sent Me while it is day; night is coming when no one can work."*

How much more should we be doing the work of our father? We should all be aware of the shortness of time and help bring souls to Jesus...now. We do not know who is watching our lives, so let us be true witnesses for Christ.

Proverbs 14:25 (AMP) says in part, *"A truthful witness saves lives."*

As Jesus said, "I thirst," let us also thirst for souls to win for the master. Let our song be, "Lord, lay some soul upon my heart and love that soul through me!" Let us also thirst that soul for thee and let me ever do my part to win.

Why This Book is Needed

So many of us go through life thinking that we are alone, feeling scared, and perhaps even wondering if anyone out there could possibly relate.

Stop wondering. Many individuals can relate. While the struggles they have gone through may be different, they are also remarkably similar in nature.

Have you ever felt so alone, and you did not think you were ever going to get through or even past the pain? Who did you talk to? Can you afford to go to counseling? Will your family help? Can you even trust anyone enough to share what is or has happened to you? Or have you burned so many bridges in the past it seems nobody wants to hear it or help?

How do you begin a healthy relationship without bringing the baggage of past hurts with you? How do I raise my children not to repeat the behavior they have seen?

Should I even get out of bed? Could someone love me knowing everything that has happened? Do you like who you see in the mirror?

While I do not even pretend to have all the answers, I pray that when you read this book, you get revelation to the questions above and even come to the realization that, I will get through this, I am strong, I am a survivor, I am an overcomer, I have a voice and I am so worthy of love.

This book is needed for one simple fact. Women who suffer tend to try to do it alone. Brokenhearted in silence while the pain consumes them emotionally, spiritually, and yes, even physically.

When a woman is strong in spirit, there is nothing she can't accomplish.

We are warriors and even warriors get wounded, but how we deal with these wounds reflect whether we rise or submit to the wounds.

> *I can do all things [which He has called me to do] through Him who strengthens and empowers me [to fulfill His purpose—I am self-sufficient in Christ's sufficiency; I am ready for anything and equal to anything through Him who infuses me with inner strength and confident peace].*
>
> Philippians 4:13 (AMP)

When "life happens" and I have a question, I like to go to the Word of God to look for answers. There it is in black and white, confirmation.

Christ strengthens me and you. I am encouraged to pull on my savior, the Lord Jesus Christ, for strength. I also have an expectation that He will do exactly what His Word says. So, open your mouth and begin to talk with Him and do not be afraid to ask for strength and then decree Philippians 4:13 over yourself. Do this repeatedly if you need to.

Please never forget you have a relationship with Jesus so just like any healthy relationship there needs to be communication between both individuals. So, speak and listen. That's right, I also said, "Listen." God is speaking to us all the time, but we get too consumed with listening to the crap in this world that we forget to connect with our Father and creator.

He is the only one who knows us. We don't even know ourselves. We think we do, but we have a lot to learn.

Once we know who we are we will not settle for less than what we are entitled to.

I am going to go off on a little rabbit trail for a minute.

I just went into the hospital for surgery and on the morning of surgery, I had to leave the house at 5:00 a.m. My sixteen-year-old daughter had taped a note in the hallway for me that on the outside read: "Please don't read until you are in the car on your way to your appointment."

So, I grabbed the note on my way to the car with my hubby and as he drove, I began to read the note:

Momma,

I'm sure you got up before me, I'm not a fan of waking up early. However!! I decided you deserve a PROPER morning greeting. You may or may not be getting nervous about today's events, considering the situation at hand. But if you do feel like you are getting too nervous or overwhelmed, I just hope you know I'm not worried at all.

There are two sides to fear...

#1 *Forget*   OR   #2 *Face*
Everything   *Everything*
And   *And*
Run!!!   *Rise!!!!*

I've always admired the fact that I have always seen you choose option #2.

You are one of the strongest people I have/will ever know in more ways than one. I'll see you later.

I Love You,

-Your Baby

P.S. There is no need to be all mushy about this note when I see you later. I love you and I'll always be your baby.

This letter brought me great joy. This letter was from my sixteen-year-old daughter.

I shared this because even though I had a great peace about me that morning, the enemy tried to get in my ear and discourage me. I was hearing things like: *The doctor is giving you a C-section so you are going to have some major healing to do; Your uterus is more than twice the normal size, the surgeon may find cancer she was not even sure and because I was scheduled for surgery she did not want to put me through another biopsy;* and other things like that. Shut up, devil.

When I got that letter from my daughter, it encouraged me to continue walking in faith that Christ is strengthening even during this storm He was there.

You see I never knew how much my daughter was watching me *rise* instead of run no matter the situation at hand. She was watching my faith walk.

Again, this book is needed to encourage those individuals who are walking through some storms and who may need to know that He is there, He will strengthen you, and He will get you through those storms.

Why I Do What I Do

A pastor once told me that when you have been delivered, it is now up to you to go out and help to deliver others.

That word that she shared with me that day impacted me more than she could have imagined.

If you had told me a long time ago that I would be ministering to other women, especially women who were survivors of domestic violence and/or sexual assault, talking openly and helping to empower them with my own testimony and the Word of God, I would have thought you meant somebody else.

I was a broken little girl trapped in a grown-up woman's body. I had such low self-esteem and I had put up so many emotional walls that it took God Himself to love me through, to show me who I was created to be.

I wanted to know all these years, "Why wasn't I important enough to stop the abuse?"

I used to think people just didn't care or maybe they didn't know how to help; maybe it was both.

I do what I do because I do care and because I now know that one word from God can change your life forever if you will allow Him to. I started by ministering and empowering other women and have been guided by the Holy Spirit to empower other churches to incorporate their own empowerment group into their church or ministry.

When we expose the enemy for the liar he is, then we can see the Truth. We are His daughters deserving of healing and wholeness and not afraid to reveal and allow Him to heal the wounds of domestic violence and sexual assault. When I was younger, I was told it wasn't very "ladylike" to fight. If I could stick my tongue out right here, I would. That doesn't sound very ladylike. It doesn't make you any less of a "lady" when you know who you are. You are an overcomer, you are a warrior, and you are victorious.

It's time to put on the full armor of God and stand victorious.

When we come to the realization of who we are as His daughters in this earth, then, and only then, will we stop settling for less than we deserve.

I am not the person I used to be. Redeemed, righteous, not by my own strength but by faith.

So, to those of you that like me thought you were a "broken little girl," you are His daughter, loved, whole, healed, strong, with a plan and a purpose for your life.

"For I know the plans and thoughts that I have for you," says the Lord, "plans for peace and well-being and not for disaster, to give you a future and a hope."

Jeremiah 29:11 (AMP)

I do what I do because there are still "broken little girls" wondering if there is hope and healing. So, to you, yes, there is. His name is above all names—Jesus.

The Process

I never thought I would write a book. I have read many books on all sorts of topics. I have read many from cover to cover and I have also started to read many only to put them down and never pick them up again. That is not to say they were not a "good read" just that they did not inspire me to feel something or touch my heart.

Don't get me wrong, I do love reading all sorts of books, but if you don't have my attention in the first few pages, then "See ya." It is my belief that the written word should take you someplace. Someplace visual, where you can see what the writer is putting into words.

Anyone out there who has ever done anything of value knows there is a process. Whether it be raising a family, starting a business, starting a ministry, or writing a book.

This book has been a long time coming. While I was in South Carolina, I would meet a woman whose faith during a tragic life event would open my heart to be ready to receive an assignment to write this book.

So many years have passed by and I will be honest, I can be lazy. I should have done this many years ago when I was given the assignment. However, I needed to go through a process before I could begin writing this book—a growing up, if you will.

First and foremost, I had to spend more time with the Father. I had to seek Him for guidance in all things. I asked Him to help me to be able to see others with His eyes. I did not want to judge others and give them my opinion. My opinion does not matter, the only thing that matters is to love others and share His love. I desired to see the end from the beginning.

Distracted

The only excuse you have is the one you make. It seems that I am on one big roller coaster of distractions versus discipline. Distractions are a constant, however, I need to discipline myself to stay focused and stay off the rabbit trail of life. So, if the enemy to my soul thinks he can distract me long enough I will forget or put off what I am supposed to be doing, that will not happen.

The thief comes only in order to steal and kill and destroy. I came that they may have and enjoy life, and have it in abundance [to the full, till it overflows].

John 10:10 (AMP)

I am fierce in my testimonies in the hope that others will be encouraged, strengthened by His Word and unfailing love, and to see us all set free from Satan's tactics. This does not mean there won't be storms, distractions, or just plain life happenings.

I must not use distractions as a reason to not complete this book. It has taken seven years since I was given this assignment and a lifetime to live it.

For the time being no discipline brings joy, but seems sad and painful; yet to those who have been trained by it, afterwards it yields the peaceful fruit of righteousness [right standing with God and a lifestyle and attitude that seeks conformity to God's will and purpose].

Hebrews 12:11 (AMP)

I am in constant training to complete the task at hand.

No more rabbit trails.

I must keep my mind obedient to the task set before me.

We are destroying sophisticated arguments and every exalted and proud thing that sets itself up against the [true] knowledge of God, and we are taking every thought and purpose captive to the obedience of Christ...

2 Corinthians 10:5 (AMP)

It seems as if every time I start writing this book, crap happens time and time again. When I announced to my husband that I was going to write this book that December, "stuff" started happening.

January: Shingles—in bed for six weeks and had nerve damage.

February: I began to hemorrhage more so than usual.

April: Surgery—partial hysterectomy, multiple tumors.

May: Dad transitioned the day before Mother's Day.

June: Mini stroke from post-operative blood clot.

July: Finances—juggling to keep our home from being foreclosed.

August: Bone pain—couldn't even be touched. Vitamin D levels almost single digit.

September: Grandbaby was 1.13 ounces when born; my daughter flatlined and was brought back. Grandchildren moved in with me.

November/December: Fatigue at an all-time low like a rag doll. Vitamin B so low I had to get injections.

January: Enrolled grandson in boarding school. Granddaughter moved four states away with Dad.

These are just a few things that happened in one year. After all of these "crap happenings," you think I would have given up. No way, not this lady! I am fierce!

Don't get me wrong, I could not have endured or survived the constant bombardments without the unfailing lover of my soul, my King, Jesus Christ, my Savior, my Peace in the storms of life.

But Jesus was in the stern, asleep [with His head] on the [sailor's leather] cushion. And they woke Him and said to Him, "Teacher, do You not care that we are about to die?" And He got up and [sternly] rebuked the wind and said to the sea, "Hush, be still (muzzled)!" And the wind died down [as if it had grown weary] and there was [at once] a great calm [a perfect peacefulness].

Mark 4:38-39 (AMP)

I knew He was always there with me even if I could not see Him, I would be encouraged by His presence and I would receive an unexplainable joy even when things seemed at their darkest because I needed to discipline (remind) myself, "God has journeyed with me through worse."

I encourage you to try to look beyond these storms no matter how difficult and yes even heart wrenching and look to Him for His peace.

And the peace of God [that peace which reassures the heart, that peace] which transcends all understanding, [that peace which] stands guard over your hearts and your minds in Christ Jesus [is yours].

Philippians 4:7 (AMP)

You will keep in [a]perfect and constant peace the one whose mind is steadfast [that is, committed and focused on You—in both [b]inclination and character], Because he trusts and takes refuge in You [with hope and confident expectation]. Trust [confidently] in the Lord forever [He is your fortress, your shield, your banner], For the Lord God is an everlasting Rock [the Rock of Ages].

Isaiah 26:3-4 (AMP)

The Lord will give [unyielding and impenetrable] strength to His people; The Lord will bless His people with peace..

Psalm 29:11 (AMP)

I am now putting my pen to paper and going forward in this journey with God and seeking His guidance in completing this book.

Where Do I Go from Here?

I would like to begin with prayer. Heavenly Father thank you for your presence and for sending the Holy Spirit to help me in my time of need. I thank you for supernatural wisdom and understanding for I cannot do this on my own accord. Thank you for always being there for me, even when I did not realize it. I thank you for an amazing opportunity to share in a relationship that I never knew existed. A relationship with my Creator that will last for all eternity. I did not earn it; I could not prepare for it; you have loved me right where I was, and you continue to do so regardless of any circumstance I may face. I would also like to thank my spiritual parents, Apostle Dr. Philip Thornton and Pastor Gwen Thornton, for lovingly raising me as their spiritual daughter. They are the ones I credit for teaching me about a relationship with God. I love and celebrate you both.

So where do I go from here? I am an overcomer. I have survived many things in my life, that I will share in the pages to follow. We were never meant to just survive but to overcome.

I have been told if you get a Word more than once and it glorifies God then it is a Word from God. I have received a Word to write this book more times than I should probably admit.

Back in 2006, I started to write about my mother, who had passed away in my arms of lung, bone, and brain cancer July 24, 2005. I did it at first because she was such a great lady and I wanted her memory to live on.

I found the process to be very therapeutic for me. Man, did I struggle. Every time I would pick up that legal pad of paper and write about her illness, I would break down. As a result, the book stayed unfinished.

In December of 2013, I announced to my husband that I am going to write a book. He lovingly smiled at me and said, "That's good honey." I said, "No, really. I want to write a book to inspire other women." He smiled again. About a month later I started jotting down some things in a journal and then it just sat until the beginning of April when I got a spiritual shove to contact a dear sweet friend. I called her and said, "The Holy Spirit is urging me to write a book." You see this is an assignment that I originally received years before and I really feel that it is time.

She listened and told me how to get started. I asked one very special thing, "Please keep me accountable." She agreed and told me my first assignment was due Friday, April 11, 2014. I asked her, "If I turn it in early, can I get a sticker?" She laughed and said, "No." (A note to my dear friend: I am grateful to God for placing you in my life at that appointed time.) I did turn the first assignment in four days early. (Seriously, I want a sticker!)

Well, life happens. She was not able to encourage me to continue with keeping me accountable. I slacked off. This is not her fault, and I am not trying to make excuses. It's the truth. The Holy Spirit continued to encourage me where she had left off; reminding me of what God has done for me and a desire to help others receive the peace and joy that can only come from Him.

I would encourage you to surround yourself with strong loving people who are going to lift you up, who will pray with you and pray for you, and people who will also keep you focused and accountable. Life is full of relationships, some are for but a season, all are meant to leave an impression on you just make sure it is an impression you can look back on with a happy heart.

Qualified? Choosing to be Transparent

I had quite a bit of questions. Am I qualified? What can I do for God? And many others just like these.

How can I serve Him? Am I good enough to be entrusted to help other women who are, or have suffered similar plights of my past? Most importantly, will I disappoint God? You cannot disappoint God. He knows all things before we even chose to do it.

First, I would like to examine how the world defines the word qualify.

Merriam Webster dictionary defines the word qual-i-fy

Verb: to give (someone) the necessary skill or knowledge to do a particular job or activity

: to have the necessary skill or knowledge to do a particular job or activity; to have the qualifications to do something

: to pass an exam or complete a course of study that is required in order to do something

Wow, that seems like an awful lot like relying on your own abilities. I am a human being and I am capable of making mistakes.

Now let's see what God has to say about whether or not you are qualified.

> *And we know [with great confidence] that God [who is deeply concerned about us] causes all things to work together [as a plan] for good for those who love God, to those who are called according to His plan and purpose. For those whom He foreknew [and loved and chose beforehand], He also predestined to be conformed to the image of His Son [and ultimately share in His complete sanctification], so that He would be the firstborn [the most beloved and honored] among many believers. And those whom He predestined, He also called; and those whom He called, He also justified [declared free of the guilt of sin]; and those whom He justified, He also glorified [raising them to a heavenly dignity].*
>
> Romans 8:28-30 (AMP)

Do I mean to tell you that everything is going to be easy and that you don't' have to put any effort into doing anything?

No, quite the opposite. While I trust and pull on the Holy Spirit for guidance and support, I study His Word, devouring the Word of God whenever I get the chance. I have been studying under an anointed man of God for the past sixteen years as of the date this book was written. He has been given the divine task of building big people.

Am I qualified?

Yep! He called me, and He is calling you as well. How do I know? Because the Word of God tells me this is true!

Well having said all of that, I had been entrusted with a ministry empowering women who are survivors of domestic violence.

The ministry began and was birthed on April 17, 2011. My spiritual dad, came up to me that morning and said, "Lisa, is there a need for a support group for women who are dealing with these issues?"

My reply was, "Yes, until you can crush the enemy completely."

He said, "Okay, it's yours," and he walked away.

Now I must have looked like a deer caught in headlights because one of my sisters in the church said, "Hey, lady, what happened to you?"

I answered, "I think I was just given charge of a ministry?"

If you had asked me what I wanted to do with my life, this would have not even made the top ten.

My spiritual mother had told me that once you have been delivered, it is now up to you to help deliver others. Wow, she is so right but how?

Whenever I want to be sure of something I go to the Word. My spiritual parents taught me that. Thanks, Mom and Dad.

Seek God on all things. Study His Word, it will never fail you.

God is not a man, that He should lie, Nor a son of man, that He should repent. Has He said, and will He not do it? Or has He spoken and will He not make it good and fulfill it?

Numbers 23:19 (AMP)

But first and most importantly seek (aim at, strive after) His kingdom and His righteousness [His way of doing and being right—the attitude and character of God], and all these things will be given to you also.

Matthew 6:33 (AMP)

As I previously stated, whenever I am not sure of what to do, I seek the advice of my heavenly Father. I prayed quite a bit and when I was quiet, God told me that while I was now entered into a relationship with Him of trust, that I would have to build a relationship of trust with the women He was going to bring to the ministry—women who are still struggling due to current or past hurts.

The way I was to do this is to be completely transparent, to share openly and honestly about my own baggage that He rescued me from, to create a safe and secure place where women can share, cry, laugh, and renew themselves.

You see, I thought I would have to have a degree and all sorts of other titles to do what God had called me to do. I was even accepted to a major Christian university for a bachelor's degree in Christian counseling and biblical studies. I would have gone into $30,000.00 of debt. I think we get so caught up in how we will approach an assignment or path, if you will, the way the world wants us to approach it that we can perhaps veer off the way God had originally desired His plan to function.

God wants to use who you are not who you were. He will renew you and set you so free that you want everyone else to know that feeling as well.

November 11, 2012, I was ordained with my husband to serve God by our spiritual Father. What an honor to serve such a faithful and loving God.

Although we did not have a huge party afterward, I believe that there had to be a huge celebration in heaven. We are stepping into our calling with willing and faithful hearts. That must make God smile.

Our testimonies are just some of the tools that we have been equipped with to share the gospel to those who have a need. When I say "testimonies," I mean testimonies. We all have more than one if you think about it. In the pages to follow, I pray that you will see how the hand of God has been there in some very tough times.

May you find His peace and encouragement to know that He loves you and desires you to be in a relationship with Him, knowing that He has and will never abandon you.

Facing the Truth

At the age of 15 and a half years old, I ran away from home. I could not take the abuse any longer. My dad and I butted heads quite a bit. He was a hurting individual and hurt people, *hurt people*. I was a teenage alcoholic and I experimented with illegal drugs. I flirted with danger and I got a thrill out of it.

Case in point:

When I was roughly 14 years old, I snuck out and went with some friends to a house party.

This so-called house party turned into almost everyone pairing up and going off into separate rooms to "make-out." Leaving myself and one other individual sitting in the living room.

This other individual, let's just call him Bob for no other reason than to give him a name for writing purposes.

So here Bob and I awkwardly sit in this dimly lit and quiet room not being able to help but hear the sound effects of lip-smacking going on in the other rooms.

Bob was much older than all of us and that should have been a red flag right there, but not for me.

Bob finally muttered a few words in between slurping back a beer, "Awkward, huh?" I replied, "Very." I then got up and made my way to the hallway where all the doors to the bedrooms were. My friend was in one of them, I knocked and asked her if we could get going now and she said, "We just got here. Go relax. We can leave in a little while."

The guy she was making out with was our transportation, so I had to stay.

I went back to the living room and sat pouting. Bob in his generosity said, "Hey, I'm bored, so I'm leaving. I can give you a ride if you want?"

Seizing what I thought was an opportunity, I said, "Sure. Can you drop me off at the pool hall?" He said, "No problem." The pool hall was up the road from my house, and it was where we all hung out.

As Bob drove, he was finishing up his beer. He pulled the car over and parked it facing the park up the hill by the pool hall.

I reached for the door handle and said, "Thanks for the ride." He grabbed my arm and said, "You don't think this ride is free, do you?"

I struggled and got free, I ran up the hill and he got out of the car. Instead of chasing me because he was intoxicated, he whipped the beer bottle in my direction and it just missed me, hitting the telephone pole all the while he was screaming obscenities.

Well, this chick right here snapped out of it and ran like crazy. I ran and hid down alleys, under stairs, and in doorways trying not to breathe too heavily. I could hear the engine of his car as he slowly drove down the streets looking for me. He finally gave up and I heard his tires screech off; I made it home safe. Thank you, God, for sending Your angels to have charge over me that night. Now I understand that as a mother our prayers help to intercede for our children. I am sure my mother prayed quite a bit for me.

I am not sure of the time-lapse, but not too long after that episode in my life, my dad and I had yet another physical altercation.

To be honest, the details of what led up to his outburst are foggy. I either said or did something to set him off. Still no excuse for what followed. If you are ever so angry by what someone said or did, leave the area and cool down.

All I remember is being in the dining room and he lunged at me and grabbed me by my neck, lifted me up off my feet and slid my back up the door. He drew back his other arm in a fist and within that moment I fought back. I did not plead and beg, "Please daddy, please," like I had done so many times before. I fought back with no words, I just took both of my arms and shoved him, so he fell back and hit himself on the dining room table thus releasing me.

I ran into my room thinking, my God I am dead now. Instead of coming into my room and finishing me off, he went out into the living room and he told my mother, "Karen, if she wanted to, she could kill me." My mother simply said, "She should have."

I must interject here; this is not a healthy or normal family atmosphere. But when it is all you know, you think it is the way everyone else lives. As a matter of fact, when you find out other people don't live this way, you are a little surprised and ticked off.

Okay, back on track. I ran away and came back, but by this time, the family had moved next door to where my dad's best friend at the time lived. A good ole boy from down south. (Their words, not mine.)

His pal, Mr. H., was a member of a secret club that hid their identity by wearing sheets. I overheard a comment that Mr. H. had a different sheet for every day of the week. Sorry, I don't think this is funny at all, it just shows the mentality of the crowd dad was hanging with.

When I moved back in, I was kept under a watchful eye.

One warm afternoon, two male Arabic friends and a couple of my female friends and I sat outside on the porch drinking lemonade and listening to music. We were just talking, no dancing, not even sitting next to one another. I remember catching a glimpse of a finger open a mini blind in the house next door at Mr. H.'s so the individual could peek at us. I jokingly said, "Uh-oh, I'm going to get it now." I had no idea just how bad it was going to be.

My dad had been on a trip and the next morning I was still sleeping when he got home. He apparently had spoken with Mr. H. about what had transpired while he was away.

My dad burst into my room, grabbed me by my arm, ripped me out of a sound sleep out of my bed, and yelled at me saying, "You had Puerto Ricans on my porch." My mom was trying to stop him, but he was already twisting my arm around and up behind my back, keeping it up there and kicking me repeatedly with his cowboy boots. By this time, my mom screamed, "Let her go!" She said, "That's it. We are leaving for good." Upon hearing this, he released his grip and went off into the living room. He did something I had never seen him do before, he cried. Mom grabbed a suitcase and began packing. I felt bad for him. I even told him, "Please stop crying. We'll stay," and, "I'm sorry."

Wow, "I'm sorry." Kids are too forgiving. I just wanted his love. He hugged me.

The following day I sat at the dining room table while my dad, my brother, and a friend were playing cards. Meanwhile my arm was still feeling the effects of yesterday's whooping. I could barely move my arm. My brother's friend asked, "What happened to your arm?" I glanced at my dad and said some girls pushed me. Dad seemed relieved that his little secret was not revealed. The friend said, "I can give you a ride to the doctor, so they can look at it if that's okay with your dad." Dad gave permission and we went.

Important fact: if you suspect a child is being abused, there is usually a body language. For example, when I was asked what happened I glanced at my dad for permission to answer. I also had not been taken to the doctor yet.

I had to wear a half cast for a while. After the cast came off, I left. I left for the final time staying wherever I could find a place, not knowing if I would have a safe place to sleep or a meal that day.

One day while staying at a friend's house, we were eating scrambled eggs. While she was reading the newspaper, I saw the front page as big as you please, and there was Bob's face staring right back at me. I must have looked like I was in shock. My friend put the paper down and said, "What's wrong with you?"

All I could do was point at his face. I said, "That's him." She said, "That's who?" I said, "That is the guy who gave me a ride home from the party. The one who tried to attack me by the pool hall."

As she and I read the details of the article, it basically stated that he had been charged with double homicide. He admittingly stated that he murdered two women that lived in his building because they wouldn't date him.

I will never forget his face as long as I live.

I am not going to sugar coat things: I was a hot mess. Just recently my husband was cleaning out our shed for a yard sale and he came in with a few items that I had forgotten even existed. One being my diary when I was about 22 years old. Wow, what a completely different person I was back then. My overall mindset was so not what it is today. I mean, I was so angry and negative. I almost didn't recognize me. I dropped the F-bomb like it was candy. I threw the diary away. Why? Because the enemy wants to remind you of your sin where God wants to exalt you.

Well, to be honest, I had never felt as if I fit in anywhere. What teenager does? Some make better choices when this so-called "identity crisis" pops up. I was not one of them. You see my entire existence up to that point was trying to get that attention from my dad that I so desperately wanted and deserved.

I look back at pictures of me when I was a baby and I see the love he had for me, but somewhere along the line, the relationship suffered. Puberty on my part, his never-ending affairs with other women, his abandoning our family just before Christmas and not returning until after Easter? I don't know.

I remember one time in my adolescence, my dad picked up my brother and me during one of these separations to meet his new girlfriend. She had children of her own and he doted on them; I remember being so hurt by this. I also remember the girlfriend going shopping with us and he bought presents for everyone.

I didn't want anything. I was hurting and so I was "being difficult." Anything that was suggested for me to get I refused and said, "No, thank you." Finally, his girlfriend said, "Here, Ron, buy Lisa these toe socks. All the kids are wearing these." (P.S. I hate toe socks. It's like getting a wedgie for your toes.)

We all went back to her place and I remember she had ducks outside of her place in a pond that I enjoyed watching. When dad took us back to mom, he told her that the kids loved the new girlfriend and the ducks and that we had the best time ever. That was very cruel and very wrong.

As I previously stated, hurt people hurt people. This is so true in my parents' case. You see, my mother did not know her worth or value for if she did, she would not have put up with one moment of hurt from dad.

My mother to me was many things at many times. When I finally grew up, she was my best friend. Now, my husband is my best friend.

You see, my mother did not know her worth or her value because of what happened to her when she was a young girl. Two trusted family members repeatedly did something to her that changed who she would become and what she would think about herself forever, altering her future relationships.

In later years, she forgave those individuals, but the damage had already run its course. How do you have a healthy relationship with your spouse if he doesn't know what happened? How do you trust anyone with that sort of information?

I did not find out about this until after my mom passed away. Dirty little secrets are just that, dirty, and they need to be brought to the light. They need to be revealed so they can be healed. The more we hold onto these hurts and secrets the more they will devour us. This does not mean you need to run up to someone and scream in their face, "You did this to me!" That could just backfire and turn into an altercation.

There is no easy way of forgiving someone except that when offenses come, we try to deal with them according to the Word of God. Forgiveness is not for the other person. It is so God can continue to heal you. God will contend with those who have hurt you.

But if you do not forgive others [nurturing your hurt and anger with the result that it interferes with your relationship with God], then your Father will not forgive your trespasses.

Matthew 6:15 (AMP)

Above all, have [a]fervent and unfailing love for one another, because love covers a multitude of sins [it overlooks unkindness and unselfishly seeks the best for others].

1 Peter 4:8 (AMP)

This is by no means a permission slip for someone to harm you ever again.

We are God's children on this earth, His representative, His church, His temple.

If anyone destroys the temple of God [corrupting it with false doctrine], God will destroy the destroyer; for the temple of God is holy (sacred), and that is what you are.

1 Corinthians 3:17 (AMP)

During one of the many fights that went on in my house when I was growing up, my dad yelled at my mother and said, "If it wasn't for that b**** in there (pointing to my bedroom), I would have never married you." Wow. Heartbroken to hear this, I fumbled for an Elvis Presley record to put on my record player and I couldn't find that record. I thought if I played one of their favorite songs, "Are You Lonesome Tonight?" the fight would stop. I never found it and now I felt as if I was the reason for their miserable marriage. Back in the day, it was only proper for a couple to get married when the young lady was pregnant. They were officially married one week before my due date.

You see, I would put on an act to be accepted. Dress provocatively, sneak out of the house when everyone went to sleep and go party with my friends. One night I actually took my dad's '72 Caddy, I was only about 14 years old, and I drove all over town with my friends and I didn't return home until the wee hours of the morning.

Because I was too tired from partying all night, I didn't want to go to school the next morning. I decided to take a kitchen knife and puncture a tire on dad's Caddy.

In the morning, my dad opened my bedroom door and I had already missed the bus, so he ordered me to get ready and he would drive me to school. As we started to drive, the tire wobbled, and he said, "Never mind, you better stay home. It's going to take me a while to get this fixed." You see, I would lash out constantly because I was a mess. Drinking and smoking are tools of the enemy for temporary fixes to real issues not dealt with.

Religious folks may feel why am I glorifying the enemy by talking in detail about these things? I am not, nor will I ever glorify the enemy. I glorify the living God I serve and the Lord Jesus Christ for redeeming the mess that I was. Messes made by my own choice and some at the hands of others.

The only way to receive complete and total healing and wholeness is through Jesus Christ.

Jesus said to him, "[a]I am the [only] Way [to God] and the [real] Truth and the [real] Life; no one comes to the Father but through Me.

John 14:6 (AMP)

If you have never accepted Jesus Christ as your personal Lord and Savior, there is no time like the present. All the therapy, drugs, alcohol, and messing around will never heal your heart. Invite Jesus into your heart to heal those things that you thought were too horrible. You can do it right now, open your mouth and repeat with me.

Father God in heaven, I come to you in the name of Jesus. I acknowledge to You that I am a sinner, and I am sorry for my sins and the life that I have lived; I need your forgiveness.

I believe that your only begotten Son, Jesus Christ, shed His precious blood on the cross at Calvary and died for my sins, and I am now willing to turn from my sin.

Because if you acknowledge and confess with your mouth that Jesus is Lord [recognizing His power, authority, and majesty as God], and believe in your heart that God raised Him from the dead, you will be saved. For with the heart a person believes [in Christ as Savior] resulting in his justification [that is, being made righteous—being freed of the guilt of sin and made acceptable to God]; and with the mouth he acknowledges and confesses [his faith openly], resulting in and confirming [his] salvation.

Romans 10:9-10 (AMP)

Now I confess Jesus as the Lord of my soul. With my heart, I believe that God raised Jesus from the dead and seated Him at the right hand of the Father. I repent of my sins. This very moment I accept Jesus Christ as my own personal Savior and according to His Word, right now I am saved.

Thank you, Jesus, for your unlimited grace which has saved me from my sins. I thank you Jesus that your grace never leads to license, but rather it always leads to repentance. Therefore, Lord Jesus, transform my life so that I may bring glory and honor to you alone and not to myself.

Thank you, Jesus, for dying for me. You took on and defeated death, hell, and the grave and gave me eternal life.

Amen.

And I will ask the Father, and He will give you another [a]Helper (Comforter, Advocate, Intercessor—Counselor, Strengthener, Standby), to be with you forever—

John 14:16 (AMP)

You see He will never leave you or forsake you, it is in His Word. It doesn't mean you won't have battles, but He is there with you.

I invited Jesus into my heart when I was seventeen and I had to do quite a bit of growing up in my walk with Christ. I had to do my part in this beautiful relationship with my Creator. I didn't take my part of the relationship with Christ seriously. It wasn't until God sent me to a wonderful church that nurtured that relationship that I began to get it.

Any relationship takes commitment from both parties. God never left my side; I left His side. I kept trying to "fix things" on my own. You can see how that worked out. Until I began to seek out time with my Creator there was an emptiness I felt. So now when these battles come, I know in my heart of hearts that I have an advocate with the Father thanks to Christ and His sacrifice for me. I pray, praise, worship, and dance for my King and I feel and receive a refreshing. All healthy relationships require both individuals to give of themselves. I encourage you to do just that. He loves you and is waiting patiently with open and forgiving arms, big enough and loving enough to carry you through eternity.

Forgiveness

Children come in all shapes and sizes; all are a blessing and a gift from God. When someone defiles that gift, I believe it must make God cry.

Child abuse is unforgivable, or is it? Father God could forgive us of all our sins, so who am I not to forgive my abuser?

When I was growing up, I had a part-time dad: part of the time he was at home and part of the time he was out and about with different women. When he was home, he was a strict and violent disciplinarian. Very rarely could you get away with anything.

If we were out somewhere and he did not approve of our behavior, then instead of taking us aside he would simply say, "Wait until we get home." Sometimes it would be a couple of hours before we would arrive home. During the car ride home, he would be singing along to whatever was on the radio, and my brother and I would be as quiet as church mice in hopes that if we were quiet enough, he would stay in a good mood. No sooner would we walk in the door from that long trip he would turn around and say, "I bet you thought I forgot, didn't you?" We would then beg and scream as he took off his belt and wrap the strap around his wrist with the buckle dangling and put our head between his knees, rip our bottoms down and beat us repeatedly with that belt buckle until he got tired or he drew blood, whichever came first. All the while, the other one of us—who was next—watched in horror, begging him to stop. It almost seemed like he would hear this, and it made him angrier. This went on periodically until I was about 14.

Other examples of the abuse were bruises on my neck from where he choked me for stacking the dog food cans on the floor next to the dog's dish where Mom had told me to put them. He fractured my elbow in three places because he thought I had Puerto Ricans on the porch and refused to take me to the hospital. A friend of the family took me to the hospital, and I said I had been in a fight just to protect him. I had a fractured elbow and wore a half cast for a few weeks as a result. When I finally healed, I ran away. I had enough.

I gave you just a few examples of what happened so you can realize that I had a lot of junk I carried with me. I believe if he had been the dad that God had intended for him to be then I would not have gone down the path I did.

Dads are a little girl's first example of how a man is supposed to act. How a dad raises his family, interacts with his wife, and provides for his family will set a standard for that little girl's expectations for their own future relationships.

We all have wounds and battle scars, but children never should. I now have three beautiful daughters and six amazing grandchildren. I disciplined my children, but I do not believe in brute force nor should you discipline your child in anger.

I volunteer at a battered women and children's shelter because God has delivered me from the misery of my past and if I can, through Jesus, help someone do the same, then so be God's will.

God has placed me in a spirit-led church that has helped me to put all that trash from the past in a suitcase and hand it over to Jesus, because He is strong when I am weak. This is one of my favorite visual lessons my spiritual Dad taught at the last service we had at our Lewis St. location.

After my mother passed from this life to the next, I tried to repair the broken relationship that I had remaining with my dad. I would call, and it was the same old thing: he would bring up the past and try to bully me in the conversation. After a while, I decided to only call on holidays, then I would only call once a year and most of the time I would only get the answering machine. Truth be told, I would feel relieved when I would get the answering machine and feel like I did my part.

My husband and I moved into our own place, and because my dad and I did not talk, I saw no need to tell him our new phone number. Then finally one day he actually called me on the phone. He said "Why the **** didn't you call and tell me your new number? I ought to knock you upside the head." My response? I just hung the phone up. He called back again and said the same thing. I hung up again. Now by the third call, he said, "Wait a minute don't hang up." I took control over the conversation this time and said to him if we were going to have any kind of relationship that we will no longer talk about the past and we will go from this point forward. He agreed after a couple of friendly reminders from me. I had to take back control from that bullying spirit.

My dad and I were talking once a week; he was waiting for a liver transplant and was on a list. He destroyed his liver from heroin addiction, hep c.

He was an artist and made beautiful paintings. Whenever we talked, I tried to speak the Word to him, and he shot me down. He often got arrogant and threatened God, so I usually ended the Word at that point, but I tried every time I talked to him.

One day, I got a phone call that my dad was in the hospital unconscious, so I traveled over 400 miles to see him.

My prayer for some time was for restoration in our relationship. I had no idea what God was about to do next. I arrived at the hospital at around 10 p.m. that night. Dad was in the medical I.C.U. where people were kept that were unconscious, on breathing tubes, etc.

The nurses allowed me into his room. He was by himself and still unconscious; it was the third day he had been like this. They had found him face down behind a restaurant in the evening in the cold October rain.

As I approached his bed, I leaned over, kissed his forehead, and I remember being flooded with forgiveness. God gave me a glimpse of how I think He may sometimes see us in our sins as fragile broken creatures in need of His forgiveness and love. If only we would run to Him instead of those "quick fixes" in our lives.

I knew at that moment that I truly forgave my dad for all those things of the past. Here's the plus: I also forgave myself.

I traveled to my aunt's house a few towns over and within a couple of days, Dad woke up. While I was spoon-feeding him sherbet ice cream, he looked at me and said, "How can you do this for me?"

I said, Because I love you like Christ loves you." He smiled and finished eating.

I no longer looked to my dad for his approval, but I looked at him as a finished work as God sees him, someone who needs Christ.

I am to be an example of God's love and forgiveness to my dad.

In the months to come, I would share my experiences over the phone with my dad about the relationship that God has for us through Christ and Dad would listen. Somehow I was always looking for someone else to lead my dad to Christ, someone he could identify with, someone with a testimony of salvation that overcame a heroin addiction.

But that apparently was not part of God's plan.

Yes, God wanted my dad to return unto Him through Christ, but not the way I was "planning."

December 3, 2013, while at church, the pastor asked everyone in the sanctuary if we had anyone in our lives who needed a word from God? Different people would say out loud who God had put on their heart and what they needed so I mentioned my dad and explained that he was a borderline believer. Pastor smiles and said, "Well, there are no borderline believers in the kingdom of heaven." Pastor asked everyone to hold hands and agree in prayer for the individuals whom we all had called out in prayer.

The next morning while I was preparing to go to the soup kitchen for ministry and while my daughter was doing dishes, the Holy Spirit gave me an unction to call my dad. The Holy Spirit said, "It's time."

I called my dad and asked how he was doing. He had me on speakerphone, so he could paint. He said he was tired. Just then the Holy Spirit gave me the words. I said, "Dad, can I ask you a question?" He said, "Yes." "When you close your eyes for the final time, what do you think will happen?" He said, "I don't know. What do you think will happen?"

I was thinking to myself, *Glory to God, is this really happening?*

I shared the Word of God with my dad with such passion in my heart. I told him that through Jesus Christ, the only one way to the Father, that all things are made new, that nothing that my dad could do through his own works could achieve salvation. No amount of money, no contracts, nothing but the saving grace of Jesus Christ's sacrifice could do this. I asked my dad if he was ready to receive Jesus Christ as his Lord and Savior? He replied, "Yes." My heart leaped with joy. I instructed him to raise his arms as a sign of surrender and I led him in the prayer of salvation.

When we were finished talking and praying, I said I have to get going for ministry at the soup kitchen. I'll call you later, love you. He said, "Okay, honey, love you too."

I hung up the phone, dropped to my knees and shouted with praise. All the while my daughter (who had been listening while she was doing dishes) said, "Was that Grandpa?" I said, "Glory to God, yes!" I was so elated. I thought if God chooses to take me home right now, I would be a happy camper.

I kept looking for others to do what he had already placed in me, a boldness that only God can grant. To be a spark of the fire of God to help others in this journey of life.

I would be remiss if I did not include the prayer of salvation in this chapter.

God wants us to be a part of His family. He doesn't throw our sins in our face. He simply wants us to return unto Him, and to walk in Sonship.

For "whoever calls on the name of the Lord [in prayer] will be saved."

Romans 10:13 (AMP)

Because if you acknowledge and confess with your mouth that Jesus is Lord [recognizing His power, authority, and majesty as God], and believe in your heart that God raised Him from the dead, you will be saved. For with the heart a person be-

lieves [in Christ as Savior] resulting in his justifi-
cation [that is, being made righteous—being freed
of the guilt of sin and made acceptable to God]; and
with the mouth he acknowledges and confesses [his
faith openly], resulting in and confirming [his]
salvation.

Romans 10:9-10 (AMP)

I acknowledge that I am a sinner and that Jesus took my punishment on the cross for my sins. He took on death, hell, and the grave for me, and Father God you raised him on the third day, and He is alive. I repent of my sins. I accept Jesus as my Lord and Savior. I accept my salvation from sin. Thank you, God, for forgiving me and giving me eternal life with you. Amen.

In the months that followed as my relationship with my dad was restored, we would have conversations about many things.

I didn't know just how much fun it would be to have a relationship with my dad.

He had been so angry at God most of his life and now he was at peace with God and himself.

The day before Mother's Day, May 10, 2014, my dad was 70 years old and in his final moments. I was in his hospital room with two others and praying over Dad and kissing his forehead. I sat down next to one of the ladies. She said, "There is something different about you. Even though you are going through this horrible moment, you have this 'peace' about you." Praise God! What she was witnessing was God's presence in that little room not only keeping me under His protective wing but there to bring my dad home.

I know in my heart that I will be reunited with my dad someday in heaven.

I thank my Heavenly Father and give all glory to Him for teaching me to forgive; for only through Him can we truly heal.

Freedom and Liberation

"Prison is prison." Out of context that sounds like an obvious statement. However, think about prison itself. You now have limited rights and privileges, if any at all. You are in constant confinement, you are told what to do every waking moment, what to eat, when to sleep, who you can associate with, and everything in between.

I personally have never been incarcerated, praise God. I probably should have been for many different reasons, but I somehow always managed to slide under the radar.

The first time I went to a prison was to minister to a woman I had never met. I had received a phone call from a friend of mine who worked in P.F.A. (protection from abuse) court. He told me this particular woman was just brought in and he gave her my card. He said that she was out of sorts and that she could really use some support. She was being transported to the county jail and had no one. She was being charged for assaulting her spouse of twenty years.

This was at the beginning of my ministry and I was a little surprised I was being called to minister in a prison. I can honestly say that many years later I am not so surprised anymore, just grateful. You see, God will direct my steps and He won't leave me without instruction.

I will instruct you and teach you in the way you should go;
I will counsel you [who are willing to learn] with My eye
upon you.

Psalm 32:8 (AMP)

My friend told me that this woman would be in solitary, and instructed me to visit her Sunday morning.

Well, I began to have a conversation with God. Yes, that's right. A conversation with my Father, He is that available for all His children. I said, "If You believe I am worthy enough to send me to minister to this woman in need of a Word from You, then if nothing else, I will be obedient." He assured me that He will give me the grace and wisdom. God is not a man that would lie.

So, that Sunday I went to the county prison and as I sat in the waiting area, I sat next to a grandmother who was waiting to see her grandchild and we struck up a conversation.

She asked me who I was visiting and when I told her I was there to minister to a woman I never met, she asked me where I got my degree from and out of my mouth flowed, "I study at His feet." I continued that all the degrees in the world are not going to do me a lick of good if I do not have the love of God in my heart. The women I minister to just want to know where I've been and how I got where I am today. Healing and wholeness; they don't care about titles and degrees, just freedom and liberation. Sometimes due to the junk in our lives, past hurts, abuse, low self-esteem, and the list goes on, we tend to put up walls to keep people out all the while becoming our own prisoner.

So if the Son makes you free, then you are unquestionably free.

John 8:36 (AMP)

What completely touched my heart was when I went to sit on the one side of the glass and watched a fragile petite woman with uncombed hair, no makeup on, who looked as if she had been crying nonstop for days, sit across from me. She had no idea I was coming. She looked at me from the other side of the glass and sat down.

We picked up the phones. She said my name and said, "I can't believe you're here to see me." I asked her why she couldn't believe it. She replied that her own family wanted nothing to do with her.

I said, "I came because you needed to know that you are not alone." She broke down and cried. I began to minister to her, and I told her of His love for each and every one of us and urged her to know in her heart of hearts that she is never alone. I saw her begin to find peace with the truth and I told her to meditate on a few Scriptures when she got back to her cell. She asked me if I would come back the next week and I agreed. She hung up her phone and she was actually smiling as she waved goodbye to me.

We are representatives of Christ here on earth and when someone is hurting, shouldn't they leave our presence feeling better than they did when we first encountered one another? Her heart was ready to receive a word from God.

So we are ambassadors for Christ, as though God were making His appeal through us; we [as Christ's representatives] plead with you on behalf of Christ to be reconciled to God.

2 Corinthians 5:20 (AMP)

When I returned a week later, she was smiling, her hair was fixed up and she was wearing makeup. She picked up the phone and recited the Scriptures I shared with her the last time we met. She was going to be transferred down south and I would not see her again, but what she told me was that she really felt she could face the journey ahead of her because she has God to lean on. She then thanked me for coming; it really made her feel loved. That made my heart smile. I left the prison feeling proud, proud of her for allowing God to touch her heart; proud of me for being obedient, stepping out in faith, and going to the prison to minister to someone I never met; most of all, proud of the God I serve. He is big enough to handle all the details needed to complete the task at hand.

I have found myself stepping out in boldness into places I never would have imagined going to.

Places like a prison, and even a strip club. That's right, a strip club. I hate to disappoint anyone here, but there is no such thing as a gentlemen's club that exploits women.

As I was driving past a well-known establishment one afternoon, I heard God say you need to go and minister to a woman in there. I hesitated and said, "God, if that is what you want me to do, I will. However, you gave me spiritual parents to guide me and not that I am trying to be disobedient I just want to make sure this is what I am supposed to do."

I asked my spiritual dad and he advised me that should I hear God's instruction for me on this. God instructed me to go with the understanding that I am not there to judge someone or to just sit and drink or watch. I am there for a divine purpose, to give him a call so he may keep me in prayer when I go.

About a week or so later, I was sweeping the floor in my kitchen when I get the word to go again. I called my Pastor and he prayed for me. I headed to the establishment with great anticipation and a passion to allow God to move through me.

I pulled up to this place and while I sat parked in my car, I prayed. I saw two individuals leave the building hanging all over one another and I asked, "Is that who I am supposed to minister to Lord?" It wasn't. I was kind of hoping it was. Pastor said when he had prayed for me earlier that I "may not even have to go in. It could be someone in the parking lot."

I approached the door and as I turned the doorknob, I entered this building no longer a little nervous, but with a confidence that He was with me.

When I walked in and made my way to the bar, there was someone on the stage, two people—a man and a performer—sitting at the bar, and a female bartender. I sat down and had to order a soda; I did not drink. I asked the Lord, "Who is it that I am here for?" The woman on stage just finished and was quickly exiting the stage to the dressing room area in the back, is it her?

I got nothing. I was glad I didn't have to go back there. Then the woman who was sitting with the man at the bar got up and headed to the stage. The man leaned over and tried to speak to me, but it sounded like a deep growling voice not making sense. I asked again, "Lord, is it one of these two individuals?" I got nothing again.

Now, I was sitting there looking around the place and saying, "God, who is it that needs to hear from you?" He directed me to the lady bartender. I got up, headed over to the end of the bar where she was standing, and I reached my hand out to her and as she grasped my hand the Holy Spirit showed up. She did not snatch her hand back from me, instead she kept looking into my eyes with tears flowing. After a few minutes of speaking to her, I released her hand and walked out of the building. I have no idea what the Holy Spirit said to her, but I pray it was enough for her to know just how much He loves her.

You see, God will put people in your life for a moment, a season, or even a lifetime to let you know He is there always and that His love is abundant.

Don't be afraid to grab hold of that hand, His hand.

Mindset/Calling

Have you ever been given an assignment or a task that, well, you just either didn't want to do or you were not sure you were even capable of doing?

I will be honest here. I can be lazy when it comes to crossing the finish line when writing this book. I believe I was going about this all wrong. I was taking on the "perfectionist attitude." This book is not going to be a struggle anymore because I need to let go and let God guide me in the completion of this book. After all, He gave me this assignment. While I was visiting in South Carolina, I met a woman whose faith helped me to open my heart.

Many years ago, on August 22, 2010, while my youngest daughter was still little, my father-in-law's cousin had just passed on. His cousin lived in South Carolina.

So, I loaded up the car with my father-in-law and my little one and we headed over 570 miles to South Carolina. Little did I know that I had a divine appointment that would change my life.

A day and a half later we arrived in South Carolina just in time for his cousin's service. We went to the cemetery and then over to the hall for the repast meal.

What happened in the next hour changed me tremendously. The widow was gracious and sweet. In my own thoughts, I was wondering how she was able to seem to be at such peace. Now I don't know what she was going through internally, but she appeared to be almost protected and peaceful.

She shared some of the details of the illness that her husband had gone through and how she cared for him. All the while never blaming God. She instead shared that because she clung to God that her faith sustained her during what had to be one of the most tragic and heart-wrenching events of her life. She seemed to have a peace about her; it was His presence that gave her the strength to carry on.

You see, up to that point in my life I had never experienced the peace that only His presence can offer.

I was profoundly moved.

Driving on the highway back to Pennsylvania was when I believe I heard God speak to me for the first time. He speaks to all of us, but I am usually preoccupied and/or just plain not listening.

Oh, and by the way for me, when God speaks, I don't hear some animated, deep voice speaking with an echo, like in the movies. I hear Him speak to me as if I am having a conversation with a loved one. After all, He is my Father.

He said, "You are going to write a book." I looked over at my father-in-law who was fast asleep in the front passenger seat, so it was not him. I heard that voice again clearly say, "You are going to write a book; these are the women who are meant to inspire."

So, of course, I did nothing with that. Did I really hear God? How can I be sure? Perhaps I am just being lazy?

Life happens, years go by. Excuses happen. Now when I heard God speak for the first time, I was beginning my walk with Him. Some people coin the phrase, "Baby Christian." I was beginning a relationship with God I never knew existed. God had planted me in a church that was teaching me the truth. Relationship, not religion. I attended church, studied His Word, worshiped, attended bible studies, power lunches, surrounded myself with others who would help to encourage my faith walk, and spent time with God.

I was called to ministry in April of 2011, and I loved being a part of something so much bigger than myself.

In December of 2013, I received an unction from the Holy Spirit, so I announced to my husband that I was going to write that book. His reply was, "Okay, you do that." My husband has always supported my adventures, if you will.

Ray is my rock. He puts the silly in my serious. He and I have been together for 24 years. Ray is the answer to a prayer I prayed a couple of years before he and I ever met. And we are still passionate about one another.

I started writing a couple of paragraphs and some notes in a hardcover notebook and then nothing. I got very sick with shingles for six weeks.

A few months later in April while I was finally laying still resting from surgery, I opened my laptop and began the process of writing this book.

I was writing about things I thought I had long forgotten. The words poured onto the pages as the Holy Spirit guided me. Glory to God. Before I knew it, I had chapter after chapter written.

God is relentless in His pursuit of us and if He gives you an assignment, He won't just let it go. He will provide you with the means to do what He has called you to do.

I was sitting in a hotel room as I was writing this chapter, getting ready to take a flight to Texas, when I was filled with awe of God. I love Him so much.

I have had many changes in my life, relationships, homes, family additions and losses, physical as well as emotional changes. The only change that I truly had to undertake was my mindset.

I had to renew my mind so that the true transformation could take place. Have you ever put on the most gorgeous looking outfit, had your hair just perfect? Only to look in the mirror and say, "Who am I kidding, I'm still...?" Have you ever put on the same gorgeous outfit, had your hair just perfect again, felt amazing almost like you were floating on air and all is right with the world? Well, for me that is what had taken place when my mindset was changed. Renewing my mind with what God says about me versus what I chose to believe in the past is what I hope shows in my transformation.

So please when you look at me, I hope you see what I now see: A woman who loves God and knows without a doubt that He loves me as well. I am His daughter made in His image and after His likeness. Perhaps I even show His love to those I come in contact with. However, don't underestimate my big heart for a doormat. I also know that I am a warrior and will not sit idle while the enemy tries to wreak havoc on others. I walk in power and authority to pray in the name of Jesus and will do so accordingly. I know this is all true and available for anyone who desires the same for themselves. For me, I believe this was the beginning of my faith walk.

He loves you and has a plan and a purpose for your life. Just spend some time with Him and He will guide if you will allow.

Describe Yourself

I was having dinner with a dear friend one evening when I heard the Holy Spirit say, "Ask her to describe herself."

When I had asked her, she described just a few attributes. However, she is so much more than who she described.

As I reflected on this conversation, I was reminded of a time about twenty years ago when a person asked me to describe myself. I replied, "Brown hair, brown eyes, and average height." Well, doesn't that describe a huge percentage of planet earth?

I joke about how I had described myself over twenty years ago because although I may battle occasionally with "self-perfectionism"—you know, where you say things like, "I should be this," "I should be that," "I should say this or that," "I should have accomplished this or that by the time I am XYZ years old"—it still plays into how I describe myself and how I walk through life.

Sometimes I can be my own worst critic until I remind myself of what God has already said about me.

For example, in Proverbs 31:10-31 (AMP) God says in part that we are valued, noble, worth more than rubies. We provide, we work eagerly, we bless others selflessly, we are clothed in strength, we are dignified, we speak with wisdom, we are faithful, blessed, honorable, watchful, creative, just to name a few.

> *He will call upon Me, and I will answer him;*
> *I will be with him in trouble;*
> *I will rescue him and honor him.*
>
> Psalm 91:15 (AMP)

I remember crying my eyes out in joy at the mere thought that God's will is to honor us and that He would be with me in times of trouble.

Going back to describing myself, I now understand a little more clearly. When I "reflect" on what God says I do not need the broken mirror image of what the world dictates or what I think I should be, look like, behave like or even dress like. My perception is now renewed and not deceived.

We have been blinded by many false images of who we are, so much so that we tend to believe the lies and try to alter ourselves to fit into these categories. All the while never truly hitting the mark of "self-perfectionism." When we now see ourselves as God sees us, then the little packages that we are in no longer limit us.

For me, it was a process of healing. A letting down my walls and truly embracing who God said I am.

God loves me and God doesn't make junk.

So here I go now to describe myself because of God and Jesus' sacrifice, I am:

Blessed, loved, healed, whole, strong, fierce, loving, joyful, thirsty to help others, righteous, highly favored, spiritually gifted, funny, faithful, loyal, creative, a woman who when I get up in the morning the enemy says, "Oh, crap, she's up again," a wife, a mother, a grandmother, a minister, an example of His love here on earth, powerful and walking in authority, and most of all, His daughter and joint heir with Christ Jesus.

Yes, I am 5'6" with brown hair and brown eyes according to what the human eyes may see. But I am so much more and so are you! We are *fierce!*

"Wander Woman"

This next chapter is "Taking Care of the Caretaker" a/k/a "Wander Woman."

I had been going through quite a lot that year, and in August, God orchestrated my trip to the beach.

I live in central Pennsylvania and the closest beach is hours away. Not to mention, my two cars were not working well and I really didn't have the finances to make a trip let alone pay someone to care for my family while I was gone. I just kept saying over and over, *I need to go to the beach.* For weeks I kept saying this. I was almost desperate in my "I need to go to the beach."

My daughter was going to be cared for by a friend, and my father-in-law would have his needs met. My husband worked third shift and could not get any time off. But my friend said she would come with me and we could use her car.

The weather report showed a 100% chance of rain on that Friday when we would get to the beach. At this point, I didn't care. "I needed to go to the beach" even if all I get to do is put my feet in the sand or look out at the vast deep ocean. "I needed to go to the beach."

My friend and I headed to Easton to my husband's aunt and uncle's house to stay overnight so he could drive us to the beach the next morning. Still, the weather report forecasted 100% rain for the next day.

We arrived at the beach and it was grey and cloudy. My friend and I got our chairs set up and began walking up and down the beach singing and praying in the Holy Ghost while looking for shells. The sun came out and it was beautiful.

As we sat down, she began reading a book she brought with her and I opened my notebook – and boom! The Holy Spirit downloaded to me the "Taking Care of the Caretaker a/k/a Wander Woman" chapter.

My friend tried to talk to me to share a chapter she was reading, and I just kept writing like I was in a frenzy. I couldn't keep up with what God was ministering to me. You see, I know that this chapter was meant for me. "I needed to go to the beach" because He needed to get my attention to receive healing in this area of my life. The beach is my happy place; His peace is my happiness.

It is my desire that it ministers to you as well.

Oh, I almost forgot. After I was done writing the chapter, I read it to my friend who stands witness of this download and the events that happened. After I closed my notebook, the clouds rolled in and it began to rain so we packed up and left the beach. We were on the beach for just a couple of hours, but this chapter has blessed me for a lifetime.

Taking Care of The Caretaker a/k/a "Wander Woman"

Have you ever felt burnt out?

Do you take care of any of the following?

A spouse, children, an elder relative, a special need loved one, grandchildren, or perhaps an ailing family member?

How about the above mentioned coupled with the following:

Running a business, pastoring a church, working full- or part-time, or perhaps all of the above?

On top of all of that, add in cleaning the house, doing the laundry, gardening, household repairs, pets, handling the finances for yourself, and an elder you may care for. Not to mention school, homework, and medical appointments to name a few. You get the picture. Sound familiar?

You may even take care of the meal planning, shopping, cooking, etc.

So just a quick question: Where are you on that huge list? You're not!

That is a list of privileges—that's right, I said privileges. Think about this for a minute. It is a privilege to be entrusted to take care of someone and/or something. However, when we don't know how to either say no or, here's the "D" word, delegate then these privileges may become overwhelming and can result in a "Burnt Out" caretaker who needs to be taken care of.

We don't have to do it all, even if we think we do.

Speaking for myself here.

I sometimes just want to take care of everyone and everything. I would think that if I want it done right, then I better just do it myself. Or I get tired of waiting for someone else to do it because after all, I know how to prioritize better than anyone else. "Yeah, right!"

I do need to rest, I do need to laugh, I do need to say "no" a little more often.

Apparently, self-guilt is not part of my genetic make-up, yet I have applied it very heavily it is ugly.

I wonder why I didn't recognize it sooner. I seem to be a self-proclaimed "Wander Woman."

You see, I tend not to get out of my own mind. I think too much and I do too much.

I need peace, His peace.

When I allow Him into my presence, there is Great Peace. Even amidst the most chaotic times. I said "allow" because He is always present. I just seem to be such a *"Wander Woman,"* wandering around with a tattered cape flailing behind me.

I need to make time for Jesus. He makes time for me; I never question that. I just tend to be a *"Wander Woman."*

We were never meant to be wanderers, to wander aimlessly. We were meant to walk hand in hand with our creator in the ultimate relationship. He holds us by our right hand.

"For I the Lord your God keep hold of your right hand; [I am the Lord], Who says to you, 'Do not fear, I will help you.'"
Isaiah 41:13 (AMP)

I have often said I have a servant's heart and it brings me such joy personally to help others. However, *"Wander Woman"* shows up time and time again. She starts new projects before completing the old ones then feels overwhelmed because now *"Wander Woman"* doesn't have just one unfinished project, but several that are heaped onto the privileges of her everyday life.

Now *"Wander Woman"* is wishing she had more help, wishing she could manage time better, wishing someone would pitch in.

I have noticed that His spirit within me tugs me back. He is my anchor and so when *"Wander Woman"* shows up, I know that Jesus, my hope and the anchor to my soul, gently tugs me back to Him where I may have His peace.

This hope [this confident assurance] we have as
an anchor of the soul [it cannot slip and it cannot
break down under whatever pressure bears upon
it]—a safe and steadfast hope that enters within
the veil [of the heavenly temple, that most Holy
Place in which the very presence of God dwells]...

Hebrews 6:19 (AMP)

Perhaps *"Wander Woman"* could ask out loud. But see *"Wander Woman"* has been doing so much for so long that it's time she takes a seat and listen to what God has to say about that flailing cape she so proudly drags behind her.

After all, He is in our every moment. Who better to consult? Ask God—what a concept, right?

People will ask advice from all sorts of people and places. Asking and consulting God is not a concept but a necessity. The Word of God is not a book, it is an instruction manual for getting through this life.

When the people [instead of trusting God] say
to you, "Consult the mediums [who try to talk to
the dead] and the soothsayers who chirp and whis-
per and mutter, 'Should not a people consult their
God? Should they consult the dead on behalf of the
living?'"

Isaiah 8:19 (AMP)

This asking, praying, and thanking God puts me in a place of Great Peace. He sent the Holy Spirit to be my helper, and yours too.

When I ask, thank, and praise, I enter a place of *peace* that the *pace* of my life is not allowed to enter. Renewing my mind and transforming me to see, think, and act in such a way that I may continue to enjoy the privileges of my days, I choose to get up in the morning and start my day seeking, thanking, and asking my creator to teach, guide, and help me to be a better, wife, mother, grandmother, friend, and disciple to the individuals I have in my life, as well as a better daughter to Him.

To end our day as a family, we pray, thank God, and ask Him to send His angels to guard us as a hedge of protection. Does this make my life perfect? Not even close.

We end our evening before going to bed with His peace surrounding us. In that brief time of prayer together we believe that we receive what God has promised. God is faithful.

For any other self-proclaimed *"Wander Woman"* out there, take the time you need to receive the peace that only God may grant.

That tattered cape can be tossed aside because He is willing to give us the robe of righteousness for that shabby tattered cape. He loves us that much.

A Heavenly Visit

January 2011, our Pastor called for a corporate fast and prayer for a seekers covenant.

We as a corporate body of believers were going to participate in a fast for eleven days and seek the face of God in prayer and worship.

Each person would fast according to what God spoke to them, some would do a liquid fast, some a Daniel fast eating only foods that come from seed, some would do a hard-fast water only, some fasted from social media, etc. I was used to going without food, but this was different, this was for a greater purpose.

During these times we prayed and sought God. During these eleven days, we all met at the church corporately to pray and worship as well. Three days into the fast I kept praying, *I want to see Your face.*

Now I have heard of other individuals who have visited heaven, how beautiful it was, and that is wonderful, but my visit was to give me information on my purpose, even though I did not realize it at the time.

That Wednesday evening January 12, 2011, after I got home from church, I went to sleep, and what happened next transformed me forever. Pastor is always saying a man with an experience is no match for a man with an argument. I share this because I experienced this very real visit to heaven.

In my dream/visitation, I looked around and saw many people wandering back and forth aimlessly in front of a huge building. I saw that the lights were on inside the building, so I entered in. I am curious even in my dreams. Once I entered the building, not far off in the distance I saw an area that had these stalls kind of like separate showers and changing rooms. Each stall had a huge fancy shower head. I then noticed one of the doors opening and there stood a lady that at the time was a member of our church. She looked completely different. In the natural, she was an elderly woman who was hunched over and relied on a cane to get around. In the spiritual realm, when she opened this door to the stall where the showerhead was and walked out. She was now standing completely erect adorned in a beautiful white glittering ballerina costume. She looked at me and smiled, even her eyes sparkled.

I went outside to speak to whom I perceived was in charge and I was face to face with Jesus. I was in His presence and He was in mine. He listened to me and I listened to Him. I had such a peace about me.

Then I woke up. I tried to go back to sleep but I couldn't. I really wanted to go back. I have never felt so much love.

> *And do not be conformed to this world [any longer with its superficial values and customs], but be [a]transformed and progressively changed [as you mature spiritually] by the renewing of your mind [focusing on godly values and ethical attitudes], so that you may prove [for yourselves] what the will of God is, that which is good and acceptable and perfect [in His plan and purpose for you].*
>
> Romans 12:2 (AMP)

What I received from this visitation was if you will renew your mind, I will transform you. Hallelujah. How awesome is that?

I did not know it, but that was the birth of the women's ministry that He would entrust me with three months later. Renewing ourselves was going to be key to no longer being overcome by our circumstances but becoming overcomers.

Ministry

If you told me that I would answer a call to minister I would have thought you were nuts. Seriously, nuts. I couldn't have imagined that I could be used to minister the gospel (good news) of Jesus. After all, I was a hot mess throughout my life.

Here is the great news: God doesn't want to change who I am, He wants to redeem me and use me to share my testimony of his saving grace to bring His light that now dwells in me to a broken heart for anyone who will receive Him.

> Since all have sinned and continually fall short of the glory of God, and are being justified [declared free of the guilt of sin, made acceptable to God, and granted eternal life] as a gift by His [precious, undeserved grace, through the redemption [the payment for our sin] which is [provided] in Christ Jesus...
>
> Romans 3:23-24 (AMP)

My pastor said it so clearly one day while he was teaching during a power lunch (Bible study at lunchtime).

And He said to them, "Go into all the world and preach the gospel to all creation."

Mark 16:15 (AMP)

My pastor explained that this verse doesn't necessarily mean that everyone is called to be a pastor, missionary, or have a ministry. The word preach in Greek (kerusso) means to proclaim, to declare, to announce, or herald a message. We are to preach to our world of influence and to those individuals we may encounter.

I know I had read this scripture many times before but sometimes I just need to have it broken down.

This means the people I come in contact with are the people I am to share, declare, proclaim, and announce what Jesus has done to set me free.

This revelation made a huge difference to me as to my spiritual value in the kingdom.

I believed up until then because of how I had been raised as a Catholic that I could only truly serve God as a nun cloistered away from family and friends. Again, this was my experience.

Sidebar – My dad brought me to a convent when I was in my early teens. While being interviewed by the Mother Superior of the convent, she knew this was not my call and said that I would not be a good fit for the life of a nun. Needless to say, my dad wasn't happy.

As I am writing this book, I asked my husband, "Do you think I could be a Nun now?" He answered, "Yes." I don't know what to make of his answer. I think it is because he believes a nun is called by God for His purpose and their obedience to God is their way of devoting themselves to be His hands in the Catholic church.

Many, many years later I was given the privilege to be a part of a ministry for women who were survivors of domestic violence and sexual assault.

So much healing had happened in the years I was part of this ministry not only for the women who were part of this group but also for myself.

You see, God used our testimonies to help offer other women hope. We had a weekly support group/ empowerment group in a secure location and shared openly discussing all topics in a someone's life that pertained to domestic violence and or sexual assault and healing. We shared, we cried, we prayed, we grew, and we healed.

There is something comforting about shared life experiences and seeing the healing in someone's life.

I had a confession of faith to have an empowerment group in multiple cities where Jesus is our core for healing. I am still hopeful.

As I look back on the women that received healing while in this group, my heart smiles. I happened upon a letter from a lady who wanted to assist with the group.

She had graduated from the group and desired to come back to the group and assist.

I asked her to seek God first and then write a letter as to why she feels pulled to be a part of this ministry.

She did just that. She wanted to give back, she wanted to be that example of healing that she received.

In her letter to the ministry she writes:

> Before this ministry, for my life, there was: medication, counseling, group therapy, which I thought were good, however, I did not feel at peace.
>
> I felt doubtful and did not trust anyone, including God. However, I knew I needed and was looking to be completely healed in my spirit.
>
> When I decided to accept the invitation to attend an empowerment group meeting, I started with a broken untrusting spirit.
>
> I felt skeptical about whether involving myself in this group would open the door that would free my bondage I was holding within my spirit.

The day I opened the door that is when the healing of bondage and strong holds of "I am not worth anything, I am not pretty, I was a bad mother, I am weak, powerless and damaged material." All of this became:

"I am beautiful, I am the daughter of the living God who created me, all-powerful to overcome the snares of my enemies who want to defeat me. I am rich and have the strength as God promised to succeed in the path that he planned for my life."

Her letter continues to say, "This ministry, anointed by God, helped empower my spirit to trust God myself and other people. Being a part of this ministry allowed me to believe in myself and find who I am; God's beautiful daughter made in his image."

She goes on to say:

God gave me a vision a long time ago which at that time I was not empowered enough to walk in that vision, and it was not the season.

Today is the season, which I want to follow and step into that vision.

Being a part of this ministry will be the vision God has for me.

Helping women understand and see in their spirit they are a daughter made in God's image understanding the beauty they have inside their spirit. I want to be used as a victorious vessel letting women see what a healed broken spirit looks like.

I am victorious. Thank you, God, for this ministry.

How humbling it is to be a part of helping someone heal. Words cannot express the joy her letter brings to my heart.

At one of our graduations, a political dignitary asked, "Is there a male counterpart to what you do?" I replied sadly, "No, not as far as I know."

Men also suffer the effects of domestic violence and sexual assault throughout their lives so there needs to be a male counterpart to provide healing for those survivors as well.

I had to ask God to help me see people as he does, to see past what my eyes could see, to see his finished work, a healed child of God.

Thank you, God, for allowing me to have been a part of your ministry. I look forward to where you may lead me next.

Domestic Violence/Sexual Assault

Definition of domestic violence: Violent or aggressive behavior within the home, typically involving the violent abuse of a spouse or partner.

The National Center for victims of crimes defines "sexual assault" as:

Sexual assault takes many forms including attacks such as rape or attempted rape, as well as any unwanted sexual contact or threats. Usually, a sexual assault occurs when someone touches any part of another person's body in a sexual way, even through clothes, without consent. In the United States, the definition of sexual assault varies widely among the individual states. However, in most states, sexual assault occurs when there is a lack of consent from one of the individuals involved. Consent must take place between two adult individuals who are not incapacitated and can change during any time during the sexual act.

Now I am sure somebody reading this is thinking, I can't believe this is in a book like this. A book of healing and overcoming through Christ Jesus with fierce personal testimonies must reveal to heal. Details are not necessary but exposing the trials that tried to keep us in darkness are necessary to bring them to the light. We are the church and we need to pray and speak healing into every dark corner where pain, shame, lies, and brokenness are curled up in a mass of devastated flesh. When we do, we stand a little taller, a little stronger, and a little happier. It's time to allow the spirit of the Lord to heal broken spirits.

Now the Lord is the Spirit, and where the Spirit of the Lord is, there is liberty [emancipation from bondage, true freedom].
2 Corinthians 3:17 (AMP)

I experienced the abuse at home growing up. The abuse was physical as well as emotional. After time, the physical would heal, but I carried the emotional from relationship to relationship.

It tugs at my heart to this day to look back on that little girl recalling what acts of violence that anger produced at the hands of my dad who was supposed to be my protector. Too many to write, too graphic to give detail the physical abuse.

I will say this though, all the insults and emotional abuse I received, I would eventually learn, I was actually owning it. I was saying those same things about myself. "You're just a girl," "You're ugly," "You'll never amount to anything." I even started adding to it with, "You're fat and stupid, and nobody wants you." So, I became a "loser magnet."

If a guy was a jerk, cruel, or abusive, chances are I either dated him or ended up married to him, current husband excluded.

Abuse is a beast. It will only thrive if we feed it.

There is something called a power and control wheel. It's a tool used to help you recognize eight different tactics that are used when there is a physical or sexual violence history. Your partner has proven before that this would be a result if you did not comply, so this is how they gain power and control. In a healthy relationship, there would be a discussion with no threat of violence if your partner doesn't get their way.

On the wheel, the outer ring reads "Physical Violence Sexual." The eight tactics inside were used in my past relationships by either my dad or exes.

Tactic #1

Using coercion and threats. Dad was the first in this violent area. We would be somewhere and get in trouble. The next thing he would say is, "Wait until you get home." No matter how long we had been out, as soon as we walked in the door, the beatings began.

Tactic #2

Using intimidation. While married to my ex, he gave me a Springer Spaniel dog. One day a friend's little boy was visiting, and the little boy was antagonizing the dog a lot. I was trying to keep the boy away from the dog, but the boy was too quick and lunged at the dog. The dog bit him. My ex picked up the dog, threw him in the trunk of our car, grabbed the neighbor, and drove off. He had the dog shot, I found out later. I also found out this monster had been beating the dog while I was at work. I was devastated.

Tactic #3

Using emotional abuse. Wow, this applied to both my dad and my exes. Dad: "The only reason I married you" (to my mom) "is because of that little *****" referring to her being pregnant for me. Exes: Name-calling, humiliating me by shoving my head in his lap in front of others, telling me I'm so ugly nobody will want me. Too much to list.

Tactic #4

Using isolation. Exes. If I was at a store and asked the man at the meat counter to repackage something, I would be accused that I was flirting and I always paid for that later. I was moved four states away from all of my family and I was only allowed to call when he was around. If I went somewhere, I had to tell him all the details because if he showed up, they better be accurate or else. I had no support system. This was before cell phones and the internet.

Tactic #5

Minimizing, denying, and blaming. Dad: Years later when we talked said it wasn't that bad. Exes: One pushed me down a flight of steps while I was pregnant with my eldest. He slapped me across the face for changing the tv station without asking permission first. Choking me until I almost passed out claiming, "You're being dramatic, I didn't hurt you."

Tactic #6

Using children. Exes: He would put my daughter to bed before I got home and tell me I wasn't a good mom. I worked two jobs. It wasn't his responsibility, only to find out he was abusing her too.

Tactic #7

Using male privilege. Exes: I worked, took care of the baby, and cleaned the house. He was unemployed laying around all day. When I would say something, I would pay for it physically. I even had to hand over my tip money so he could gamble.

Tactic #8

Using economic abuse. Exes: I worked a full-time and part-time job, handed over my paycheck. I had to beg for a dollar to get a soda at my second job. He took care of the finances and never let me have an account of my own. Get this, I made more money than him. When we separated, I got my first checking account. I cried when I got my temporary checkbook, although I only had $10 in that account.

If any of these circumstances are going on in your life, contact the National Center Against Domestic Violence, www.ncadv.org. 20,000 calls are placed a day to domestic violence hotlines. 182-gun related domestic violence fatalities from January 1, 2018, to April 17, 2019, and counting. Ten million people a year are physically abused by an intimate partner. 20% of women in the U.S. have been raped.

There is help available. The first step may be the hardest, but it's the most important one you can take. They can help you put a safety plan in place. I've made a copy of a safety plan available in this chapter.

The safety plan is a plan on how you will respond to future violent incidents. Enlist family, friends, and co-workers, if possible, to help with your safety plan. If your life is in danger, tell the advocate on the phone or in person. I pray that you are safe and know that you are loved. May God's healing embrace surround and comfort you through your journey of healing.

Example of a safety plan:
When I have to talk to the abuser, I can

_____.

When I talk on the phone with the abuser, I can

_____.

I can make up a "code word" for my family, co-work-ers, friends, and counselor so they know when to call for help for me. My code word is_____.

When I feel a fight coming on, I will try to move to a place that is lowest risk for getting hurt, such as _____(at work), _____(at home) or _____(in public).

I can tell my family, co-workers, boss, counselor, or a friend about my situation. I feel safe telling

_____.

I can screen my calls, texts, emails, and visitors. I have the right to not receive harassing phone calls, texts, or emails. I can ask friends, family members or co-workers to help me screen my contact. I can ask these people for help: _____

_____.

I can call any of the following people for assistance or support, if necessary, and ask them to call the police if they see the abuser harassing me.

Friend: _____

Relative: _____

Co-worker: _____

Counselor: _____

Shelter: _____

Other: _____

When leaving work, I can _____.

When walking, riding, or driving home, if problems occur, I can _____.

I can attend a victim's/survivor's support group with the Domestic Violence program, like

_____.

Contact Information I need to have:

Police Department: _____
Domestic Violence Program: _____
Sexual Assault Program: _____
Attorney: _____
Counselor: _____
Spiritual Support/Clergy: _____
Probation Officer: _____
Other: _____

Remember to clear your search history on your computer and phone. If possible, leave a copy of important documents with a trusted friend or loved one. Gather and leave a change of clothes that won't be missed with the trusted support person.

Remember there is a way out carefully.

Additionally, there is a list of National Hotlines in the back of this book.

Along my journey of healing I have been fortunate enough to meet Lisa. The minute I met her I knew we had something in common. You see, for years we were survivors of horrific relationships and now we are overcomers. What was once our ceiling is now our floor. Standing strong on the promises of God. Healing in all areas of our lives because of the greatest sacrifice of all, Jesus. As you read Lisa's story, please recognize that God has taken back what the enemy tried to steal, and we won't be silent. Too many suffer in silence. Thank you for sharing.

In this next chapter, I came in contact with a true warrior and a very dear sweet friend who shares her experiences to offer hope to others.

Married to the Devil

I am fifty-one years old and I am from Pennsylvania. I am of Italian descent and I was raised in the Roman Catholic Church. I attended Catholic school from kindergarten to twelfth grade. (Need I say more?) I had wonderful parents and loving siblings, I, being the youngest of four.

I had a pretty normal childhood up until I was about 11 or 12 years old. I had an uncle who started molesting me around that age and it changed the fun-loving, athletic, excellent student into someone I did not know. My grades started dropping and I could not focus in my basketball games. When I was about 15 years old, the molestation stopped.

I never told my parents because I knew my dad would kill him. It was his brother who molested me. I have forgiven him and moved on with my life, but I believe it is the reason I have no desire to be with Caucasian men intimately.

Fast forward to when I was eighteen and in the United States Army. I joined the Army with my college sweetheart when I was eighteen. I was two weeks ahead of him in training and we were both supposed to go to Germany. I got to Germany two weeks before him and while I was in route to Germany, his orders were changed to Hawaii without my knowledge. This was in 1985 before cell phones and the internet. I was pregnant but did not find out until two months after I arrived in Germany. By the time we caught up with each other, three months had passed. Although we were engaged, he did not believe I was pregnant with his child. We broke the engagement off and when I was about seven months pregnant, I met my future husband.

I met him in the non-commissioned officers club across the street from the base and we started dating days later. He was an atheist and I was still going to mass when I could, but it was sporadic. Long story short, I had a girl, whom he treated like his own daughter. When she was about six months old, I got pregnant with my second child, our daughter, and we got married.

About two years into the marriage, he became mentally and physically abusive and drank alcohol excessively. I allowed him to gain control of me somehow.

He told me I was ugly and no one would want me with two kids. It lowered my self-esteem.

The physical fights were bad. I grew up with all boys and I can fight so when he would hit me, I would hit him back. These fights were very bloody. This happened in front of the kids. We were both still in the Army, but I was in the process of getting out because my contract was up. At this time, the girls were two and one years old.

I was not able to spend quality time with them, so I chose to get out and I became a personal trainer and a gym manager.

The abuse continued off and on for about fifteen years. It would happen once, then not again for six months to a year, so I dealt with it praying he would change. I always thought about leaving, but he apologized, and things would go good for a while until he drank alcohol then here came the cruel words and the slaps in the face.

The girls were A-B students, played basketball, soccer, softball, tennis, and volleyball. From the outside, we were the perfect family. We had the cars, the boat, the house, all the material things a person could want. Our friends admired us, and no one knew of the abuse. They all loved and respected my husband.

He was a top non-commissioned officer with many achievements. He retired from the Army in 2000 and became a police officer. He worked twenty-four hours on, forty-eight hours off.

In 2003, he quit drinking and we were back to being best friends again. Things were going well. I was managing the gym, going to school, and starting a cleaning business. I was busy, to say the least. We went camping, hiking, fishing, and boating with our friends and all our children. He was working one day on and two days off, we split all the household duties, cooking, etc. I got off at nine pm, so I picked up our oldest daughter, who was a senior in high school and star basketball player, and he picked our youngest up from tennis practice at five pm. Life was good...or so it appeared.

I got home from work about 9:30 pm and as soon as I was pulling in, I knew he was drunk, and a fight was inevitable. I could feel it and it was obvious. He and four of his friends were sitting out front and all of them were intoxicated. This was after a year of him not drinking any alcohol at all. I just said, "Hello," and went inside to see the girls and eat dinner. A few hours passed, and he came inside. I was in the kitchen ironing. He picked a fight with me almost immediately. I do not remember what the fight was about, but it escalated quickly into him hitting and choking me and knocking me to the floor with the ironing board. My oldest daughter jumped on his back and he got her off and started choking her. I got up and pulled him off her and I had so much strength I pushed him out of the door with such force it ripped off his shirt. (Ironically, it was a wife-beater t-shirt.) I got the keys to his truck and threw them out to him and dialed 911 for the first time after fifteen years of abuse. He fled in this truck with nothing but what he was wearing and without his ID.

I had marks all over my neck, a black eye, and blood coming from my nose. We waited scared, crying. I knew this was the end. I could not take it anymore.

The girls were in high school, in their junior and senior year; they were seventeen and eighteen years old. I was not going to subject them to it anymore. The police came, wrote a report, and took pictures of my neck and face. They told me if he returned to just give them a call.

He stayed gone all night. I had a cleaning job that morning. It was Saturday, so I woke the girls up and told them to call me if he came home.

Before I got to the job, they called and said he was home. I turned around and I called 911 and let the police know he was home.

When I arrived home, I went in and the girls were crying. I asked them what was wrong and where he was. We had a huge storage shed in our yard we had fixed up as a spare room with a TV and games, etc. They told me he was out there. Again, I asked, "What is wrong?" and my youngest daughter said, "I have to tell you something, Mom." I said, "What?" She said, "Dad has been molesting me since I was twelve years old." (She was fifteen now.) I felt like the life had been sucked out of me. I fell to the floor. I said, "What?" and we all cried and hugged each other. I re-called the police and told them what happened.

A single plainclothes detective came to pick him up. He asked my daughter what he did, and she told him. He went to the shed and brought my ex-husband out handcuffed. It was devastating, to say the least. It was the darkest day of my life. I felt like my heart was ripped out of my chest. I could not breathe. Our lives changed in a flash.

The detective took him to the station, and I had to take our daughter so she could give her statement. He was arraigned the next day. The things I heard in that courtroom no mother should ever have to hear. The things he did to my sweet innocent child, who is such an awesome girl. She was an honor roll student, star tennis player, had a boyfriend. I couldn't have asked for a better girl. She is amazing.

I went down to my knees in the courtroom. I could not believe that the man I was married to for seventeen years could do this to our precious child. How did I not see it? Why did she not tell me sooner? So many things were swirling in my head. Everyone loved him and re-spected him. He was a police officer, respected by his peers. He was awesome sober, but alcohol opened the demon door, and him being an atheist turned the thunderstorms into hurricane.

She did not tell me because he told her if she ever told, he would kill us and burn us in the house. A demon.

He was held with no bail until his trial date six months later. He pled guilty and was sentenced to fifteen years with no parole.

Our friends and family were devastated. I have never seen so many men cry. His friends were in disbelief that the man they admired and looked to for advice could do this to his own child. His family thought she made it up. Our lives were changed in an instant.

I quit the gym business because it was just too much to deal with. I wanted to die or quit. I couldn't sleep or eat and went from 135 lbs. to 110 lbs. I looked horrible, felt horrible, but I refused to let the devil beat me again. I was in the process of buying the gym I had managed for ten years and had two weeks left until the deal was final when this happened. God closed a door, not just a regular door, a dream door. Owning a gym and becoming a massage therapist have been lifelong dreams. I continued with my cleaning business and built my clientele. I refused to give up.

I started going to church again thanks to my good friend, Elijah. I got saved in November of 2004, and my entire life changed. Not long after I got saved, I got a federal security job on a U.S. military base. God opened a better door for me due to my military experience. It led me to travel the world. I did five years there and then went to Kuwait for two years. I came home again for a year, then I went to work in Kosovo and Afghanistan for three and a half more years. It was a huge sacrifice. I missed a lot of time with my family, but I overcame every obstacle thrown in my way.

He had credit cards in both our names taped under the dashboard of his truck with over $75,000 worth of debt on them that I knew nothing about. He was a master manipulator. He had the bills going to a P.O. Box. He was using my credit score of 847 to get these cards and forging my signature. To no surprise, they were all maxed out.

God opened the door to allow me to do government contracting overseas so I could pay off all of the credit card debt. I met a wonderful man who now treats me like a queen and has showed me how a woman is supposed to be treated. I went back to school and got my massage therapist license. I was off for two years going to school and I had a hip replacement, so I went back to Afghanistan for a year to become debt-free.

Now I am home to do my true purpose, my dream job as a massage therapist. I am a healer and God brought me back to heal His children. It has been a long and difficult journey, but I grew into the woman

God created me to be. If you are facing a similar situation, do not lose hope. Stay positive and focused. You can achieve anything you desire. I have wanted to be a massage therapist since I was six years old and look, now at 51, I am. Trust and ask God to lead you in the paths you should go.

Ask Him to close the doors that need to be closed and open the doors that need to be opened. Step out in faith and walk through the doors He opens like the Queen God created you to be, not the victim of your situation.

Relationships

Relationships take work, and some take more work than others. Have you ever heard the expression, "You get out of it what you put into it?" In my experience, that hasn't always been the case.

I sometimes tend to put into a relationship more than I ought to, giving too much of myself thus becoming a doormat or an enabler not what I initially intended. Not knowing the right balance in a relationship can be tricky. To me, it can be like walking on a tightrope, picture if you will a tightrope walker with their arms level on each side of their body as they balance themselves on the rope. This keeps their body balanced for the task. Leaning too much to one side can cause disastrous results.

Both parties need to know the proper amount of give and take in a healthy relationship. "Healthy relationship." What a hopeful term. A term that quite honestly can at times be difficult to achieve. Especially if the parties involved have their own agenda, i.e., what can "I" get from this relationship? There are many types of relationships, family, marriage, sibling, dating, friendship, business/work, to name a few.

Relationships differ from person to person. As for myself, I had a pretty good relationship with my mother and yet I struggled to have a healthy relationship with my own daughters. I would either do too little or too much. Sometimes not knowing when to just listen or let them fall down and learn from their mistakes. I guess I just wanted them to know how much I loved them. I would either be what they considered "too critical," or all up in their business. My heart would ache for them each time they suffered whatever that pain would be or whatever storm they would be in the midst of. You see, I thought I could "fix" everything, I could help them "avoid" problems in life by either sharing what I had gone through or by sheltering them too much. That backfired.

At times, they would actively seek those things I told them to avoid. At some points, they'd actively embrace exactly what I wanted them not to or stay clear of completely because I knew it would lead them down the path of further suffering. I desired a relationship with my girls that it be one of them feeling comfortable enough to talk to me about anything without feeling apprehensive.

One of my daughters said to me, "Mom why is it you refer to scripture when there is a problem I talk to you about?" I told her it's because that is where I have found the answers to my problems and the peace I need to get through the storms in my life.

You see, I kept wanting my daughters to have the kind of relationship with God that I have. While they can have a beautiful relationship with our Father, each relationship is unique to that person. No two relationships are the same.

They may consist of some basic components like communication, intimacy, love, respect, and the like.

They are still unique to the individuals involved so regardless of how, "I" wanted them to have the type of relationship with God that I experience, they need to have their own intimate experience with Him.

One of my daughters told me that she didn't feel she could come to me with problems. That broke my heart. I never wanted to be the person that pushes them away from Him. I, however, will not agree with a mess either and say oh, that's ok.

Others had tried to do that to me for a good portion of my life. I did not know what a beautiful thing it is to have and enjoy an intimate relationship with my Father.

Our relationship with Jesus is that of reconciliation, not religion, that God was reconciling the world to Himself in Christ not counting people's sins against them.

> *That is, that God was in Christ reconciling the world to Himself, not counting people's sins against them [but canceling them]. And He has committed to us the message of reconciliation [that is, restoration to favor with God]. So we are ambassadors for Christ, as though God were making His appeal through us; we [as Christ's representatives] plead with you on behalf of Christ to be reconciled to God.*
> 2 Corinthians 5:19-20 (AMP)

Definition of reconciliation: the restoration of friendly relations.

Reconciliation involves change or an exchange in the relations between us and God or between ourselves.

It is my prayer that my children enjoy that beautiful exchange in their own relationships, with God in their own unique way as He has already set before them, and for them to know how much I love them.

Big Daddy Ray

"Big Daddy" is a term of endearment I use for my husband, Ray. Big Daddy was a prayer answered two years after I prayed for him.

I had been in an abusive marriage and remember one evening while my then-husband was upstairs sleeping, I was standing in the kitchen sneaking a cigarette and leaning out the kitchen window. I was looking out into the evening sky at the beautiful moon through the leaves of the tree. I remember praying, "Dear God, where is my Prince Charming? Please send me my knight in shining armor. This can't be what you meant for me to live like."

In April, two years later, my then-husband and I separated for a week and out of pressure from him and a promise to change, I went back to him. I figured I would give him one more chance.

Meanwhile, in June, the most beautiful man entered my life.

I didn't know it at the time, but he was going to be my husband for life.

I was the assistant at the place of employment he walked into for an interview.

I saw him and said quietly to myself, "Please let this man be my interviewee and not a customer." Sure enough, this 6'1" broad-shouldered, light-eyed, wavy-brown haired, pretty-smile Adonis was here for the interview.

After about forty-five minutes of the preliminary interview with me, I asked if he had a minute. I went out and told the manager that he should come in and talk to this guy. I said he is very nice, great communication skills, he's strong so no trouble lifting, very funny, and really cute. The boss laughed and said, "Well, if he's cute then we need to hire him." All jokes aside, he got the job, not because he was cute but because he was qualified.

We worked together for six months. I was his supervisor so we never let on to the other one that we liked one another.

I was still married and really struggling in that relationship. The abuse had gotten worse and I had enough. I had started to plan how I would be able to leave. After all, he controlled everything in my life.

He controlled the finances while I worked two jobs. He wasn't paying the bills. He would get angry if I asked for any money to buy a soda at my second job.

I had no idea how to pay bills. I trusted he took care of all of it—He didn't. We almost lost the house, so he wanted me to work at a strip club to earn the money. I didn't. I chose to borrow the money from a relative and I paid it back after our divorce that I also paid for on a payment plan. We slept in different rooms for most of the last year of our marriage and I exercised, drank coffee, smoked cigarettes, and worked two jobs. All the while not knowing the nightmare I was in and that my daughter was in as well. He would abuse her while I wasn't home, threaten her, and put her to bed before I got home.

When I told her we were leaving, she cried. I didn't know the extent of the abuse she suffered.

Many years later when she felt safe enough to tell me, I was infuriated. She said she forgave him and didn't want to press charges, nor did she want to relive it again.

Her future relationships were tremendously affected by this.

When I finally found an apartment, one that I could afford, I had to orchestrate everything just right as not to put up a red flag to my soon to be ex.

I was so stressed out, so much so that during December of 1996, I lost fifteen pounds in less than a week. I finally got the courage to leave and the landlady agreed to allow me to give her $50 extra a month to go toward my security deposit.

December 10th, while at work, Big Daddy saw the stress I was under. We went for a ride and after pulling the truck over, this nice guy asked, "What is going on? You look awful." I just blurted out that I was leaving my abuser and I was getting an apartment. He offered to help in any way he could.

Big Daddy was a very patient man. God definitely hooked me up even though I didn't recognize it then.

After I moved into my new apartment with my thirteen-year-old daughter, Big Daddy would try to give me things for the apartment and I would turn it down because in my past experiences "things came with obligations." I had so many walls up I almost locked out the man that God sent me, a patient, compassionate man with strength, love, and courage to grow old and to grow in faith together.

I got a promotion and an opportunity to move back to New England. When I told Big Daddy I was leaving to take the promotion, he said, "I can't lose an angel like you. If it's okay, I am going to move to New Hampshire too. I'll get my own place and a job there too." I had no idea how much this man really loved me.

One evening before I moved to New Hampshire, Big Daddy and I were sitting in the living room and having a conversation while listening to music, you know the kind of conversations that last until the early morning hours. He said, "I'm going to marry you someday." Wow, I'm thinking to myself, after all I have been through in my past, how awful I am at marriage, an abuser magnet, all the things I now know that I am not. How could he say something like that?

I felt this sudden rush in my body as if I were going to let go of all of my bodily functions. I felt lightheaded. I smiled sweetly at him and excused myself to head to the bathroom. I started to walk through the kitchen from the living room and before I knew it, I was back on the sofa and he was rubbing my face and asking me, "Are you, all right?"

Apparently, I had fainted on my way to the bathroom and he carried me back to the living room. I was so embarrassed. I apologized and told him I don't think I am "marriage material." He knew otherwise.

I took the promotion and Big Daddy moved with me.

I did something different in this relationship. We expressed our expectations to one another, our wants, our dreams for the future as well as what we would not tolerate. I even told him of my past abuse. I thought once he heard all of that he would be gone in a flash. He said that he cannot believe just how sweet and strong I was in-spite of those things, things that others would have used as a reason to be bitter.

At first, I had a problem with our age difference, but he didn't. I am six years older than he is, but I guess I didn't look it. Thank you, hair dye!

Big Daddy is the silly to my serious. We do balance one another out.

When Ray (Big Daddy), met my side of the family in New Hampshire at a cookout the first reaction from my aunts was, "Oh my goodness, what has Lisa gotten herself into now?" Ray was wearing a muscle shirt, shorts, sunglasses, and he had a goatee. He was standing there looking very intimidating and because of my past hook ups, my aunts were fearful he might be abusive too.

As my one aunt now puts it, as soon as Ray started talking, they fell in love with him.

God sent me a strong, yet loving and compassionate man. He sent me a man that would stand by my side, a man who would joyfully ride the roller coaster of life with me with both hands up; a man that would remind me to put my hands up too, even when that ride hit its peak.

My mom was a worrier and I guess I picked up that trait. Ray would remind me through the years that I should not worry about things I cannot control, whether it be finances, children, or whatever the situation!

> But first and most importantly seek (aim at, strive after) His kingdom and His righteousness [His way of doing and being right—the attitude and character of God], and all these things will be given to you also. "So do not worry about tomorrow; for tomorrow will worry about itself. Each day has enough trouble of its own.
>
> Matthew 6:33-34 (AMP)

I would sometimes worry myself sick, so I needed reminding. Stress and worry can affect your physical body as well as your mind.

> *Do not be anxious or worried about anything,*
> *but in everything [every circumstance and situ-*
> *ation] by prayer and petition with thanksgiving,*
> *continue to make your [specific] requests known to*
> *God. And the peace of God [that peace which re-*
> *assures the heart, that peace] which transcends all*
> *understanding, [that peace which] stands guard*
> *over your hearts and your minds in Christ Jesus [is*
> *yours].*
>
> Philippians 4:6-7 (AMP)

Ray has been a gentleman through and through. We have been together for almost twenty-four years now. He treats me like a queen, and I treat him like a king. While we may argue from time to time, we never degrade one another, we never throw our pasts in one another's face. We have learned that sometimes it's best not to say something just to get it off our chest, especially if it's only going to make ourselves feel better and not be productive in our marriage. God is the center of our relationship. He has to be. He hooked us up.

I am so in love with my husband, my best friend. I look into his eyes and my heart skips a beat. When he holds me in his arms, I just melt in his strength; when he kisses me, he ignites a passion within me.

Now mind you, life tries to interrupt moments in our lives, but we continue to be each other's best friends because after all, when the children grow up and move out on their own, it will be the two of us growing older together, so we should enjoy each other's company now.

Who better to spend the rest of my life with than the man God sent me to spend eternity with?

I deserve God's best for me, and my husband deserves God's best for him.

I love you, Prince Charming, my Knight in Shining Armor.

The man who truly is the example of:

Husbands, love your wives [seek the highest good for her and surround her with a caring, unselfish love], just as Christ also loved the church and gave Himself up for her.

Ephesians 5:25 (AMP)

My husband made me a card for Valentine's Day. He found the words online, but he made me a red cardboard frame for it. The card reads:

My Wife,
Your life on this earth has been a blessing to so many a soul
My dear wife I hope that is something that you already
   know
I know what your life here has meant to me
It has been a blessing sent from God, that I truly see
In you I see a delicate but strong person

In you I see a loving and kind person
In you I see a sharing and giving soul
In you I see a wise and valued friend
In you I see a very beautiful woman
In you I see a very moral person
In you I see a woman who is my best friend
With you I feel the softness of your heart
With you I feel the commitment of true love
With you I feel you sharing your strengths to support me
    and lift me up
With you I feel valued as a human being
With you I feel wisdom so great and beyond your years
With you I feel the beauty that God has placed in your soul
With you I feel that you are truly my best friend, my life
With you I feel blessed to be your husband and to have you
    as my wife
You are the picture and example of a perfect wife
A person that we are all so blessed to know in our lives
It is you and your love that has changed me
God through you has shown me who I need to be
The message I see through you from God above
Is that through you God has filled my heart with love
I just want you to know that I realize that I have been
    blessed so true
That I know now that God loves me, and he has shown me
    that through you
So please believe that I feel so free and in love with you

That to God I promise I am his and then yours and always
   true
I promise to you my devotion and the rest of my life
Because with you I have a God sent gift, a beautiful wife

*A God Sent Gift A Beautiful Wife
by Danny Blackburn pub. 12/2008

This is one of my most treasured possessions. My husband poured out his heart to me. Even though he got these words online, they helped him to convey what is in his heart. Poem: A God Sent Gift A Beautiful Wife by Danny Blackburn published December 2008.

I love that he knows that it is God who has blessed us and that he puts God before me, as I do him.

God has shown both of us through Him what love and relationship resemble with God as the foundation of our marriage.

It didn't start out that way, however, it will last through eternity together forever.

Mom

Not everyone is blessed enough to have had the close relationship my mother and I had. Although growing up I did not appreciate all that she sacrificed for us.

My mother was the third oldest in a family of nine children, six girls and three boys.

My mother never completed the eighth grade, she was dyslexic and left-handed. The schools did not know that she was dyslexic, so her schoolwork had suffered, and she struggled. She told me how a teacher had wacked her hand with a ruler when she would try to write with her left hand. She helped to care for her younger siblings and never returned to school to complete her education past the 8th grade.

As a teen and possibly before, it was revealed that Mom had been violated by more than one trusted family member. She would soil the bed on purpose in hopes to keep the individuals from further attacks, and as punishment for the bedwetting, she was made to sleep in the bathtub.

When Mom was old enough, she took a job babysitting for a woman who was divorced.

One evening as my mom was at this woman's house, she answered the door. She said she looked through the peephole before opening the door and saw the most beautiful eyes looking back at her. They were my dad's hazel green eyes. He was there to date the woman mom babysat for. Somehow, he and Mom hooked up. Mom was sixteen.

Mom kind of skipped over some details like exact dates. She told her parents that she was married when she wasn't. They disowned her because she was sixteen when she left home to "marry" my dad. I believe she did it to escape the abuse at home and found herself unmarried living with dad and now pregnant with me in 1965.

Many years after Mom passed, I told dad about her abuse at the hands of two trusted relatives and he said he never knew.

He, however, added his own brand of abuse, physical and emotional. He said, "How can someone enter into a relationship with a secret like that!"

I told him, "You have no idea of the torment she lived with. You were supposed to be her knight in shining armor, instead he turned out to be another dragon in her already tormented castle.

There are so many reasons why we hide the pain and suffering from others. Shame that the abuser told us was ours, that if people knew they would hate or ridicule us further, that it's all our fault, that we are filthy because of it! That they would do to our loved ones what they have already done to us, they would kill us. This list goes on...

The enemy wants us broken to hide in the darkness he created. Glory to God, let's expose the enemy for who he is: a liar and the father of lies.

God has the victory, so stand strong. No matter what has happened in our lives God is with us so hold on to His unfailing hand for His strength.

As the years went on, the abuse continued and the cheating on my mother by my dad only added to her already low self-esteem. He abandoned her time and time again leaving her to try to figure out how to support my brother and me.

She went without quite often so that we could have something. I remember she felt bad that we had to live off PBJ sandwiches because it was all she could get for us. For years I would get stomach cramps whenever I ate one.

Mom was a very generous person. She would give even though she had very little.

I remember her driving in a blizzard on the highway. I watched as she pulled over to help someone whose car was in a ditch. On a different occasion, I watched as she ran across a busy highway to help a truck driver that had rolled his tractor-trailer.

When someone was sick or had just had a baby, she would help cook, clean, shop, or just help in any way she could.

At one point, Mom broke up a fight in a bar between two men. The men were in the bar and she got them to go outside. When she was standing between the two men to break up the fight, the police showed up. Thinking Mom was part of the fight, the officer grabbed Mom and, as she put it, threw her to the ground, cuffed her, and yanked her by the cuffs to her feet; Mom was under arrest. She spent the night in jail.

This was after my parents had been divorced in the early 1980s.

Mom had been extremely depressed and had turned to drinking. She looked for answers, but only found heartache and depression.

My mother dated after her divorce, but never remarried.

Years later when my dad was homeless and strung out on heroin, my mother and her fiancé took dad in allowing him to live in the second-floor apartment in the house that her fiancé owned. She helped dad get clean, got him to the VA to get meth treatments. She helped to clothe and feed him even when he had heroin seizures. How many of us would have done the same?

Mom was a very forgiving person, sometimes bordering on being an enabler

Mom loved Christmas. She shopped all year round with the financial help of my aunt. She and my grandmother would hit clearance sales and then Mom and her fiancé would help wrap everything for them to give out at the family Christmas party. Mom gave so much to so many.

After Mom had passed away while going through Mom's letters, I happened upon my most treasured inheritance, her letter to God professing her need for God's strength. She gave herself to God and asked what she could do for God.

8-15-87

God my life is yours to keep. I know you put me here for a reason. Please show me what I can do for you. I know that will make me happy and keep me happy.

Please forgive me for all my unforgiving sins, please.

Thank you for still loving me. Thank you for everything in life.

I'm sorry that I have to ask you for your strength and patience and understanding. Thank you.

As I read and re-read her letter to God, at first, I saw pain and now I see the joy she knew by thanking God for his strength and patience and that he had a plan or reason for her being here that it would make her happy and keep her happy.

The Lord is my strength and my [impenetrable] shield; My heart trusts [with unwavering confidence] in Him, and I am helped; Therefore my heart greatly rejoices, And with my song I shall thank Him and praise Him.

Psalm 28:7 (AMP)

Mom, until we are reunited again in the presence of God, I will continue to share the legacy of your faith. I love you and I am so proud of you.

Loss of a Loved One

December 26, 2004, I received a phone call that would eventually break my heart.

I was three months pregnant with my third daughter resting in bed next to my husband that morning when the phone rang.

It was a call from my oldest daughter. She said I have "Buddy" (a name she called my mom instead of Grandma) on the other line. She wants to talk to us at the same time.

When Mom got on the line in a three-way call, Mom said to us that she had been diagnosed with stage-four lung cancer back on November 17th. She kept that a secret from us so as not to "ruin" the holidays.

I right away said, "Mom, we have an extra room and you can stay here, and we will take care of you while you get treatments."

She refused saying, "You guys are expecting a new baby and need the room for the baby. Besides, I don't want to be so far from the family in New England."

I told her, "Mom, you're being selfish." I didn't mean it in a mean way. I was trying to convince her to come to Pennsylvania so that I could care for her. My mom was one of the most unselfish people I have ever known. I just wanted to do right by her.

Flashback to September 2004, Mom was using a cane at our wedding. She said doctors said it was arthritis. When she and my dad walked me down the aisle together, she had to do so from inside the church door because she could not step up into the church without help. During the reception, Mom would not rest. She had her own video camera and was trying to record the reception. She was in so much pain and yet she never complained.

Mom stayed at our house after the wedding for a couple of days. We found out later that while she was getting ready and packing to return to Massachusetts, she fell over her suitcase. Her hip was in severe pain. She said all she could do was lay there and cry. She only told us all of this months later after she told us about the cancer.

After hearing the news of her diagnosis and feeling helpless I did what I usually do. I put on my "big girl panties" and made a plan. My husband, our seven-year-old daughter, and my pregnant self lived over four hundred miles away from my mom, so I had to try to coordinate our lives, school for our daughter, and meals while I would be away off and on, not to mention my prenatal care.

I would drive back and forth to Massachusetts to help my mom however I could. She was having excruciating headaches. I would help her in and out of the tub and shower in the hopes the hot water would help. I would also massage her feet and she would sometimes get relief from the pain.

I remember lying down next to her and she put her hand on my now showing pregnant belly. When she did, the baby kicked for the first time. We were both elated. My husband and I had given Mom our bed to sleep in while she stayed with us that February. It was also close to a private bathroom. It just made more sense. We wanted to make her as comfortable as possible. I secretly hoped she would have stayed, but she didn't.

I was taking a nap in the soon to be nursery when I heard my mom yell out. When I opened the door, she was trying to pull herself up onto the big comfy chair in my bedroom. She had slipped in the shower and said she had been calling for me as tears ran down her face. I felt horrible. Part of me felt that maybe she would have stayed if I could have prevented her from falling or taken better care of her.

Not true she went back home to be close to her parents' siblings and to be cared for by the doctors she was already familiar with. Mom flew back to Massachusetts that February in 2005, still suffering excruciating headaches. When she got back to her house, she tried to eat something, but the pain was too severe, they took her to the hospital.

They tested her and found the cancer was now in her brain and her hip. The doctor said they were very surprised she survived the flight. Mom never left the hospital bed again. In March on one of my many visits to be with her, we met with a surgeon who said her hip ball and socket joint were hanging on by a thread, the cancer ate most of the bone away. He gave Mom hope that she would walk again. She never did.

After her surgery when they brought her from the recovery room to her hospital room, I laid as quietly as possible in the lounge chair next to her bed, so she wouldn't be alone. Mom was struggling and moaning, so I called for the nurse. Thank God I was there. Mom couldn't reach for the call button. The nurse came back out of Mom's room and said, "Your mother had an 'episode' and we gave her a nitroglycerin tablet under her tongue. We are moving her to CCU downstairs to better monitor her." I grabbed everything in her room and followed her gurney to CCU.

A few hours later at roughly 7 am, Mom was awake and in a great deal of pain from the surgery and too frail to press the morphine pump every fifteen minutes, so I helped to press it for her. I pressed the pump and said I was going to go get a cup of tea and I would be right back. Well, when I returned in about ten minutes, to my surprise the doctor that had been her doctor for years and was the one who diagnosed her had visited her and left, leaving her in tears. I asked what happened and she said Dr. N. said he doesn't believe she is in that much pain. That was the last time he ever saw her. I was furious. I said, "Mom, he just doesn't know what it feels like to be in your position and to be dealing with what you have gone through. Mom, I believe you." I pressed the pump for her again.

At that time, my aunt came in to visit with Mom. I stepped out and went looking for Dr. N. Luckily for him, I could not find him, so I went to the head nurse and told her he is not allowed back into my mother's room. I also wanted them to get her a different physician.

I had to return to Pennsylvania a few days later leaving mom in the care and watchful eyes of my family. I tried to get my Mom to go to the Dana Farber Cancer Institute in Boston. I had her all set to be transferred there once she was discharged from the hospital, but

Mom didn't want to make family travel into Boston. When they discharged Mom from the hospital, they sent her to a nursing home for physical therapy.

Mother's Day 2005, I wanted as my gift to drive up and visit with Mom. I made her a photo family tree blanket with her photo, my brother's photo, my photo, and photos of our kids, my grandkids, and even the ultrasound picture of my little one who was only two months away from delivery. I had called Mom the morning of Mother's Day from my cell phone to wish her a Happy Mother's Day. She had no idea I was in town to surprise her. When I walked into her room, she was so happy. She loved the blanket. I hung it on the wall in front of her, so she could see it from her bed.

Back home in Pennsylvania on a call with Mom, she said that she was interested in trying an experimental chemo pill that costs $2,800 for one pill. I looked up the information on it, told her the side effects, and she still wanted to try it.

When I went to visit again, her skin was like raw hamburger meat on her arms. The nurses were using an ointment that seemed like it was just feeding it. I asked, if my mom was okay with it, if I could try some corn starch instead and they said that's fine, but they won't be able to do it.

Mom agreed, and I would gently wash her arms with warm water and a mild soap, dry them and apply the corn starch heavily. I did this for three days and her skin returned to normal. This was one of the side effects of the pill.

Mom had been moved to a private room in the nursing home on the fourth floor with another hospital bed in the room for the family to spend the night. Hospice was eventually called in.

I have to say my mother has to have the most wonderful siblings. My aunts and uncles helped my brother and I come up with around-the-clock schedule, so Mom would never be alone in her final days. At the very end of May, the beginning of June, I stayed in the room with Mom for a couple of weeks sleeping in that bed and caring for Mom, brushing her teeth, fixing her hair, giving her massages, playing her favorite music. My big fat gorgeous pregnant belly and all.

One day Mom's CNA was in the room and a disco song Mom loved was playing and the CNA said, "Oh, that's my husband's song."

I replied, "Oh, he likes disco too?"

She said, "No, he is one of the original singers for this group." She said, "He now works in the nursing home downstairs." So, I pulled her aside and asked her if she could ask him if he would consider coming to Mom's room to sing a song for her. She said she had asked him before and he always refused only because if you do it for one, then many would ask. Then he wouldn't be able to get his work done and it wouldn't be fair to say no to the others.

Not much longer after that while I was in Mom's room with her and some other family members, a bunch of nurses and floor staff came flooding into Mom's room. I was a little confused by this invasion until he walked in with his wife, Mom's CNA. She introduced her husband and he sat in a chair next to my mom's bed. Mom was smiling from ear to ear. He said, "Hi, Karen. Do you know who I am?" She nodded yes. He said, "I heard that you are a fan of my music and I would like to sing a song for you if that is okay?" He said, "I would like to pray with you first." He held her hand and prayed. He then sang Amazing Grace so beautifully that there wasn't a dry eye or nose in the room except for Moms. She was frail and held a washcloth up and swung it around with joy. He and his wife, Mom's CNA, hold a special place in my heart now and forever.

Mom hadn't been out of her hospital bed in months, so one day a commercial for shampoo was on and Mom said, "I would love that."

I said, "What would you love?"

She said, "An actual shower." I checked with her nurse who got permission from the doctor for Mom to be lifted by some contraption into a shower chair. Mom's nurse wheeled her into this huge shower room and Mom made me stand in the room while this lady showered Mom.

Mom had always been modest when it came to nudity. However, at this point in her life that was the least of her concerns. When she was done, she said, "Okay, it's your turn." By this time, I had a huge pregnant belly. I agreed. Now mind you, this is just a big shower room with no privacy curtain. There was nothing I wouldn't do for Mom, big naked pregnant belly, butt, and all. This was Mom's way of caring for me. She knew I had been taking hobo baths in her bathroom sink and I could use a hot shower too.

I was getting closer to my due date and I had to go back to Pennsylvania for another amniocentesis to see if the baby's lungs had formed for an early delivery. Before my first amniocentesis, I was told there was a one in forty-four chance she would be born with Down Syndrome because of multiple factors. However, the first amniocentesis results came back as a false negative. Later at the age of ten, she would be diagnosed as "high functioning autistic." She is an amazing little girl, now teenager, and she is not a diagnosis.

My due date was July 16th and the doctors were not giving Mom long, so our family came up with the following schedule, so Mom would never be alone. After I left to go have the baby.

8 am to 4 pm: Aunt Renee would be there daily along with any other family members.

4 pm to 8 pm: My brother would come after work.

8 pm to 8 am: My Uncle George would sleep over in the bed next to her.

I gave birth on June 24, by induction, and named her Laila Karen in my Mom's honor. On June 26th, new baby in hand, we traveled from Pennsylvania to Massachusetts to lay her in my mother's arms for the first time.

Within a couple of weeks Mom's health took an extreme turn and I returned to her bedside with my newborn in a Moses basket. We stayed there around the clock during the last week of mom's life. I would pray with Mom listening because, at this point, she could no longer speak and was very emaciated. Her last words to me were "I love you." Cancer is like the enemy. It comes to kill, rob, and destroy no matter who the person is. They are finding new cures regularly and it is my prayer that cancer will be a disease of the past. Mom never gave up hope. Even though her body was giving out, her heart and faith remained strong.

I remember singing the "You are my sunshine, my only sunshine" song to Mom while I would rub her head. How I wished she would have never had to suffer like this.

With her family surrounding her, my mom took her last breath. Her CNA was in the room with all of us. I gave the CNA the baby to hold and I crawled into my mom's bed and held her in my arms as her nurse took her blood pressure. Watching the numbers on the machine drop we all held our breath. Her nurse confirmed that Mom had passed. While still holding Mom in my arms I trembled and kissed her forehead and cried so hard. My tears poured out like a flood onto Mom's forehead. I felt so broken. I felt as if a piece of me had died that day. My mom meant the world to me.

I won't lie, it took quite a bit of time, but God placed people in my path that would help me heal my broken heart.

We were never meant to experience sickness, disease, or death. None of these things were in the Garden of Eden. Here is where it gets better. This is where we as believers in Christ Jesus have hope.

Now we do not want you to be uninformed, believers, about those who are asleep [in death], so that you will not grieve [for them] as the others do who have no hope [beyond this present life].

1 Thessalonians 4:13 (AMP)

Jesus came and took on death, hell, and the grave so that we who believe may have right standing with God and receive eternal life through Christ Jesus. When Jesus had risen, He entered into the locked room a week after the apostles had seen Jesus and told Thomas about it. Thomas did not believe Jesus had risen and that the apostles had seen him. When Jesus appeared again in this locked room, he allowed Thomas to touch His wounds. Then:

Jesus said to him, "Because you have seen Me, do you now believe? Blessed [happy, spiritually secure, and favored by God] are they who did not see [Me] and yet believed [in Me]."

John 20:29 (AMP)

Now faith is the assurance (title deed, confirmation) of things hoped for (divinely guaranteed), and the evidence of things not seen [the conviction of their reality—faith comprehends as fact what cannot be experienced by the physical senses].

Hebrews 11:1 (AMP)

Jesus is speaking:

I assure you and most solemnly say to you, the person who hears My word [the one who heeds My message], and believes and trusts in Him who sent Me, has (possesses now) eternal life [that is, eternal life actually begins—the believer is transformed],

*and does not come into judgment and condemna-
tion, but has passed [over] from death into life.*

John 5:24 (AMP)

My faith assures me that my mother and I will be reunited in Heaven again. She believed and received Jesus Christ as her Lord and Savior as I do. Mom, until we see each other again I will continue to share my legacy of my faith with others. Love ya.

Along my journey of healing from the loss of my mother and just three months later, I met a woman and now a dear friend who openly shares her testimony of her husband's passing and how God kept her sheltered and covered during this time in her life. May her story inspire you.

His Embrace

I was born on August 8th, 1950, in South Dakota. When I was a young girl, my family moved to Pennsylvania.

I grew up in a dysfunctional home with an alcoholic father and a mother who never acknowledged the "elephant in the room." She just went about as if nothing happened. Seeing this I never learned how to deal with my emotions.

So, when I married my first husband, I would have anger explosions when things would get tough. I would nag my husband who was a good financial provider. I just didn't know how to love. I had not really received love from my parents, so I didn't know how to love back. They never hugged me or told me they loved me growing up. A child should experience these things.

When I would nag my husband or overpower him in a verbal explosion, he wouldn't talk to me, so I would become even more overpowering and he would go into a shell leaving me to be the one in charge in the relationship. Staying in a marriage just going through the motions and before I knew it, I found myself in the arms of another man.

I was a surface-Christian at best. I had always loved the Lord. I was going to church but only getting the basics. I now had two children and when they grew up, my husband and I divorced. I loved my family and felt abandoned. I had never been single before. I had to learn to provide for myself instead of being able to rely on my husband financially.

I got my G.E.D., which was a struggle for me. I had worked ever since I was 19 years old. I had to stop looking for someone else to care for me and learn to allow God to guide my path.

At this time in my life, I started attending church still looking for someone to take care of me all the while needing to renew my mind. What I have learned is there is still a saving grace and that is worship! Worship for me is an intimate place where just God and I are in each other's presence. When His presence is surrounding me, it strengthens me, it tears down walls, it guides me and covers me with peace and a renewed mind.

I met my 2nd husband at a teen challenge event. He saw me and kept asking my friend questions about me, so I told my friend to go ahead and give him my phone number.

We started dating and about three months in he asked me to marry him. We got married at the church we were attending in 1998. We had a lot of good times in our marriage.

We started attending a spirit-led non-denominational church where the truth about a relationship with God and not basic religion were being taught.

So, here we are, in our new church and my husband stopped attending church. He seemed to change after we married almost overnight. He started treating me differently. I asked him why and I had no idea that he was battling sobriety. Whenever he was late coming home, I thought he stopped at a bar. This was a flashback of what my dad had done in the past.

He certainly didn't share that he was trying to battle this alone he was trying to hide it from me. A mutual friend confided in me that he had been drinking again. Anything hidden in darkness can, and will, have power over you. We could have worked through this together. I think because of the situation with my dad and his alcoholism he just didn't know how to reach out.

He was diagnosed with stage four melanoma. As he began his treatments, I was hearing nurses, co-workers, and many others telling me he was going to die that I should just make plans for his service.

Just because I was hearing and seeing this attack on my husband in the natural, it was contrary to what the Word of God has taught me. I needed God's peace to surround me to keep me safe, to keep me under His wings, to keep me still during this storm.

So, I continued to worship in spirit. If it was not for God's protection, I would have not been able to get through.

I had never been around sick people like this before. God provided relatives, friends, and church family to help with caring for my husband at home while I worked.

He took a turn for the worse and had to be admitted to the hospital. Tuesday, December 6th, a friend took me to dinner while his daughter was with him in the hospital. I returned to the hospital after dinner to discover that he had passed with her by his side. It comforted me to know that his daughter who loved him was there and that he was not alone.

At my husband's celebration of life service, I felt good, believe it or not. My husband loved to see me dance and worship for God.

I chose to worship, praise, and dance at my husband's service. I danced for my husband and I danced in the presence of our savior, Jesus Christ.

God is my safe place. I can feel His love for me as I worship my Lord and Savior.

I now focus on the Word of God and I am learning to rest in His presence. I am resting in Him no matter what. I am no longer looking to man to fix me, but instead I'm looking to the One who created me and knows me better than anyone ever could.

I was there on the day of her husband's service. I personally witnessed her worshipping her God knowing that He had kept her in His Embrace while she cared for her husband, during the service, and the months and years that followed. She continues to worship and look to the Lord for His guidance, His protection, and His love to grow and sustain her. Thank you, my dear sweet friend, for openly sharing what God has done for you. I thank God for you. It is your worship in the midst of adversity that has helped to heal a part of my heart as well.

Birth and Children

Growing up I watched a TV show that had two "perfect" parents with a house full of children. You didn't see the violence or dysfunction that was going on in my own home represented on tv back then, with a part-time dad who, when he was home, was not the loving "TV dad."

I thought that when I grew up things would be different. The reality is that it wasn't. Because of the choices I made and some that were thrust upon me, I ended up a teenage mom. I was seventeen when I had my daughter. I was so not ready to be a mom and she suffered because of that. I kept trying to be her friend when she really needed me to be her mom. Children need structure and boundaries. They will make their own friends. I kept looking for a daddy for her only to fail time and time again, so we both faced lots of rejection and violence.

She is now a grown woman with children of her own and still struggles with the past. Even though she has told me that she forgave my ex, the hurt from the past still lingers in her heart. I continually pray that she may receive healing and recognize the beautiful woman that she is.

I have often wondered why we, as a body of believers, (at least to my personal experience) as the church, never dealt with the issues that so many of us have faced. I have heard of sermons, if you will, talking about healing, of your body, mind, and spirit. Healing for addiction, pornography, and much more. It wasn't until a visiting Pastor, and woman of God called out what I had thought I had hidden so deep for so long that I knew in my spirit I just needed to be healed. I will never forget the moment I released the torment of what I had done. I am not judging anyone here. I am simply sharing what I went through and what it took for me to get set free from and not permission to ever do it again.

I was stuck in a very private prison, one which only I held the key to. I had to voluntarily hand the key over to Him to help me open that prison door. If only I could forgive myself and allow Jesus to set me free. Permission was key to my healing, permission to forgive myself.

By the time I had given birth to my second child, I had already terminated three pregnancies, two of which my ex-husband did not want. When my now-husband, whom God definitely placed in my life, came along, I never even thought of getting pregnant.

In my mind, how could God ever bless me with a child again after what I did? I viewed myself as a murderer.

This is a hot topic. Although a woman has a right to her own body, an unborn child gets no say in the matter. There are so many options available to women now, too many perhaps. There are people who cannot have children and would surely love to give that baby a home. Regardless of how this baby was conceived, this is still an innocent baby.

Hear me clearly: I am not passing judgment. I just wish now that I would have chosen adoption. At least those babies would have had a chance. This broke my heart for decades. I thought my heart would never heal.

But God, He is certainly big enough to heal even that broken heart. I still held onto that broken heart for many years even after I was blessed to have two more daughters. I lived with that guilt and shame. Self-loathing. I was at church one evening and a woman of God did something different. She did an altar call for any woman who needed to get set free from the pain, guilt, and shame of having an abortion. This may seem strange to some to call something like that out for healing at church, but God is not playing when it comes to His children needing healing.

Wow, my heart ached so much at this point in my life that I didn't care who saw me walk up to the altar. I desired healing. For me to achieve this, I had to hand this final piece of my broken heart over to God. I have said for years I have given many things from my past over to Jesus, but I thought this was just too painful to hand over, too ugly, too unforgivable. He said, He would carry not some but all.

Come to Me, all who are weary and heavily burdened [by religious rituals that provide no peace], and I will give you rest [refreshing your souls with salvation].
Matthew 11:28 (AMP)

As I made my way up thinking, "Oh, man, my church family now knows my innermost shame." Guess what? They didn't care about what I had done. They cared about how much my heart needed healing. You see, I had given my sins over to God to heal all but this. I thought this was just too much for Him to forgive, so I held onto the pain. News flash, I was not the only heartbroken woman at the altar. I thought I would be. I don't know how long I was prayed over after I confessed and asked Jesus to forgive me and heal my broken heart. All I know is the pain, guilt, and shame that I carried are no longer there. It is my hope that I will be reunited with those children in Heaven.

When I found out that Ray and I were expecting a baby, I was so excited. The pregnancy was a very difficult one. At two months pregnant, I hemorrhaged and was now one centimeter dilated and put on bed rest for a week.

At three months pregnant, the day Princess Diana had died while watching the news on TV with my then thirteen-year-old, I squeezed her hand so tight I could hear her bones grind. I was in extreme pain with a sharp knife-like pain in my abdomen. I went to the bathroom and thought for sure I lost this baby. As I looked back into the toilet, I saw a very tiny fetus, my heart sunk. We lived far from the doctors and Ray was at work, so I called, and they said to bring in the fetus, so they could confirm. We lived in an Old Victorian home on the second floor. The toilet was always running, and the water swirled it away.

Upon my examination by the doctor, they said it could have quite possibly been the baby's twin, but without it, they could not confirm. However, the pregnancy is still intact. Sometimes the stronger of the two will survive and the one that is not thriving the body will reject, according to the doctor. All I know is that my daughter held on, so back to bed rest for another week. When I went back to work, I was not allowed to do anything but sit and supervise.

October 31, 1997, the doctor put me on bed rest until the date of delivery. I had to lay on my left side and drink a gallon of water daily.

February 14, 1998, I gave birth to a beautiful baby girl, 7.8 ounces. She was not breathing and there was no pulse. As this lifeless precious little one lay on the table, the nurse began working to resuscitate her. I kept asking "I don't hear her crying. Is she okay?" The doctor kept trying to distract me. The nurse would describe to the doctor what she was doing and then she would say, "No response. CPR. Oxygen." Then he said, "Cc's of epinephrine." As she injected it into her first thigh the nurse said, "No response, doctor." The doctor instructed her to administer another, so she injected her other thigh and let me tell you our little peanut let out a scream. Ray took pictures, my mom was there, and while they were reviving our baby girl, her big sister had come in and watched this lifeless little one revived.

When Ray and I had our second daughter, my mother was battling cancer. I would drive back and forth to Massachusetts from Pennsylvania to help care for my mom.

When they moved my mother to hospice in the nursing home, I stayed in a bed next to her for two weeks. My family set up a schedule so she would never be alone while I traveled back to Pennsylvania to have the baby.

I was really going through some extreme challenges emotionally.

I was on a high dose of anti-depressants. I was constantly driving back and forth to Massachusetts by myself and pregnant.

The doctors said Mom didn't have much time, so my doctor checked to see if the baby's lungs were formed yet and they said it looks like they were, but wanted to give it another week and then check again. They had me wait another week and scheduled me to be induced, so my mother would meet her granddaughter. After 19 hours, I gave birth to a healthy 6.1-ounce girl.

The next day we were discharged from the hospital and got in the car and traveled from Pennsylvania to Massachusetts on that hot June day. We stopped every hour to take the baby out of her car seat to massage her and for me to walk and stretch. I had an adverse reaction to the epidural causing my body to swell tremendously. I basically had no ankles due to the swelling. We finally arrived to see Mom at the nursing home in this heatwave. There was no power for the elevators, so we walked up four flights to Mom's room and laid her granddaughter and namesake in her frail hands.

About two and a half weeks later, I drove back to be by Mom's side bringing the baby in her little Moses basket and for the last six days of Mom's life, we never left her room.

Every time someone would leave Mom's bedside in tears, we would hand this baby to them and she brought a smile and joy to them. I could not see it then, but even in the midst of one of the most heartbreaking times of our family's life, God was there bringing joy to others through this sweet little baby.

> *Peace I leave with you; My [perfect] peace I give to you; not as the world gives do I give to you. Do not let your heart be troubled, nor let it be afraid. [Let My perfect peace calm you in every circumstance and give you courage and strength for every challenge.]*
>
> John 14:27 (AMP)

I love and cherish each of my children.

I Am Not a Diag-
nosis

Growing up I was a healthy child. I had the usual childhood illnesses, bumps, bruises, stitches, and even fractures. Overall, my general health was good.

As an adult, my health changed dramatically. I ended up with an ulcer which was the result of anorexia. I started with symptoms of fibromyalgia in 1993 that progressively got so bad that my body would give out. There were times I could not walk. I would go into bouts of depression and feeling guilty I could not care for my family.

People would hug me, and I would cringe because it felt as if I had been hit with a baseball bat. My husband would get looks because people thought he was the reason I was in such bad shape. He has never raised a hand to me. I felt as if I had a flu almost daily, chronic fatigue like a rag doll, chronic pain, couldn't think clearly, severe memory loss.

Maybe I was a hypochondriac? For a while, doctors would say it's all in your head. The craziest things would run through my mind. I knew that my body was under attack, and finally there was a name for it. The problem is that this attack overlaps many other diseases like lupus, chronic fatigue syndrome, myofascial pain syndrome, IBS, complicated migraines, etc. I was told all we can do is try to "manage this chronic illness, there is no cure." They call it the invisible disease. According to the doctors. I was told this is a lifelong illness.

I'm sorry, but I refuse to buy into the hopelessness of "this is going to be your life until the end of your life," that the doctors try to spout off, or become discouraged at how many times I have been in the hospital.

Do I do things a little differently than I used to? Yes, I try to eat right, I try to exercise, I try not to stress about things that are out of my control, and I also try to gain knowledge about this disease. Know your enemy.

The latest challenge has been memory function. While I have been journaling, it has been a lifesaver in taking back what this disease is trying to steal from me. I had a doctor tell me that being pregnant is the best thing for me because the pregnancy hormone helps the body fight back. Say what? Not a lifelong option clearly.

I was told at the age of thirty-five that my insides were like that of a sixty-five-year-old woman and that I was going to end up in a wheelchair—not very hopeful.

I almost bought into the lie. While doctors were agreeing with my body, I would continue to fight. I am not my diagnosis.

Don't get me wrong, there were days where I struggled to even get out of bed. But God, this is what I would say when a physical attack would come on.

As long as I have breath in my lungs, I choose to believe that I am healed regardless of what doctors say I stand in agreement with the Word of God healed by His stripes and not let a diagnosis rule my life. This doesn't mean symptoms don't try to pop up.

I saw doctor after doctor, specialist after specialist, test after test, endless bloodwork, MRIs, cat scans, x-rays, and different medications that would leave me feeling worse than I did when I wasn't taking anything. I took a medication that made the memory loss worse.

One day driving my daughter somewhere that we had been many times before, I literally had to pull the car over and call my husband. I didn't know where I was. At other times, I would be talking to someone and trail off in the conversation then return to the topic once again. This really scared me. I had the neurologist take me off the medicine. Only to find out later they took it off the market.

I remember taking muscle relaxers and pain killers just to try to ease the pain. I could not function. I remember feeling so helpless. I sat there with drool coming out of one side of my mouth, another drug gave me tremors, and another gave me tinnitus (a ringing in my ears). I was diagnosed with something I had never even heard of, fibromyalgia. That was in 2001, after eight years of thinking I was going nuts. Many times, I felt if only people could see the physical pain I was in perhaps they would better understand. I remember my legs gave out from under me while I was at a beauty salon with my daughter. I tried to compose myself, but I wacked the tray that had her curlers in it and they went flying in the air. I was embarrassed, to say the least.

Fibromyalgia attacks in many different directions and I have experienced a multitude of these.

Pain areas: in the muscles, abdomen, back, or neck. Pretty much all over and my hips would lock up or my legs would just give out and I would fall. This made it very difficult to run or exercise. Not very graceful.

Pain types: can be chronic, diffuse, sharp, or severe. I have also had nerve damage to the left side of my face and calves.

In February of 2017, after my second bout with shingles in three years, my face began contorting to where my chin twisted all the way up to my left ear. Yikes scared the crap out of the technician in the hospital.

She was performing a test on my carotid artery when my face contorted so bad, she got another tech to stand by my bed and she ran to get my nurse.

I could only whisper out of the side of my mouth. I saw my husband stand there watching me, feeling helpless. I whispered out of the side of my mouth "Jesus." My face began to relax again a grateful tear rolled out of the corner of my eye.

Pain circumstances: can occur at night or during the day.

Gastrointestinal: constipation, nausea, or passing excessive amounts of gas, fortunately, I have been spared the excessive amounts of gas issue. I did deal with IBS until I changed my diet and after I had my gallbladder removed.

Whole-body: fatigue, feeling tired, or malaise. Just lying there like a rag doll.

Muscular: muscle tenderness, delayed onset muscle soreness, or muscle spasms.

Sensory: pins and needles, sensitivity to cold, or sensitivity to pain.

Mood: anxiety, mood swings, or nervousness. No mood swings, just anxious that these attacks would happen in front of others who wouldn't understand what was going on.

Sleep: difficulty falling asleep or sleep disturbances.

Cognitive: forgetfulness or lack of concentration.

Hand: sensation of coldness or tingling.

Head: Migraines, skull pain, and mysterious bumps that would not pick up on an MRI with contrast.

When I was diagnosed, doctors would say it's all in your head. Are you crazy? All in my head? There were times I just wanted it to end. All the tests, all the doubts.

Here's the kicker: Over three million cases are diagnosed each year, not to mention "experts" say there is no cure, only treatments to manage it.

Imagine being told you have a disease that can sneak up on you at any given moment and never knowing what each day may hold?

I tried just about everything on the market to "manage it." That failed. All this sounds pretty hopeless, right? Wrong, I refuse to give up hope.

I remember after a stay in the hospital, I was back at the gym and the individual that was with me said, "Slow down. I can't keep up with you. Why is it that people who just get out of the hospital feel they have so much to prove?" I told her, "You don't understand. It's not that I have anything to prove. It's that I can walk and exercise and to me, that is a miracle. The fact that I am functioning today is a miracle. I will push on because every time I press on is another bruise to the enemy's ego and proof that we serve a living God who offers hope and strength even in the toughest times."

The Lord is my strength and my [impenetrable] shield; My heart trusts [with unwavering confidence] in Him, and I am helped; Therefore my heart greatly rejoices, And with my song I shall thank Him and praise Him.

Psalm 28:7 (AMP)

I sometimes need to remind myself: You are stronger than you think, never give up hope. So wear that crown, girl.

I will ride a horse again, and I will run in a marathon.

Thank you, Lord God, for holding me by my right hand through this journey.

My current trial will not keep me from my calling. Please hear me clearly, I never want pity. I just want to shed some light on a disease that even mystifies doctors.

I continue to fight the good fight of faith. Utilizing the Word of God, prayer as my key, with my gloves on and my crown straight. That is how I fight my battles.

Along my journey of healing I came in contact with a dear sweet friend, who shares her testimony in this next chapter as a letter to herself entitled, "Dear Younger Me."

Dear Younger Me

I decided to write this letter to you because you are going to face a hardship soon that will shock you and change you in unimaginable ways. You will be pushed to your physical, mental, and spiritual limits that will make your life feel like it isn't worth living anymore, but I promise that you will get to the other side and be enormously blessed.

It's the summer of 2016, and God has just called you and your amazing husband, to move out of state over an hour away from your hometown and family. You are scared and excited about the move and working hard at your new job in this new area that will soon be called home. The day after you come home from vacation with your family, you will have your wisdom teeth taken out. All goes well, standard procedure, and you will recover nicely, and your mouth will heal beautifully. In the six weeks following your surgery, your ability to digest certain foods will become increasingly more difficult. You will think that it's just because of the antibiotic, but I promise you, it isn't.

This is the hard part; this is where we get to the big stuff. So, we go through a lot of pain from here on out. As I am waiting for our gut to balance, every time we eat gluten, dairy, or eggs, the pain becomes so intense that I will feel like the walls of our sanity get a little too thin. After the surgery, I started to develop pain in my abdomen that felt like someone was squeezing my spine in my low back with the pain reaching around my sides to my digestive area where I would experience pain I have never endured before. My belly would become swollen from the pain, I could hardly concentrate on anything. I just curled up on the couch or the floor and hope that this feeling would subside soon.

I honestly waited too long to see a doctor; I was just hoping that this would all go away. I figured I would be fine if I just worked harder, was smarter, was better. My husband finally took me to the emergency room where we waited six hours to be seen by a doctor. Needless to say, we were very unhappy to finally see a doctor after all that time along with the loss of my original urine sample just for the "cramping episode," as I call them to pass and for them to determine that nothing was apparently wrong with me. At least it wasn't an issue that needed dire attention like an appendicitis or something like that—that's what I kept telling myself anyway.

Now the tables turn and thankfully in my favor, but I remind you, this is still not an easy journey and it's certainly still not complete.

About five days after the frustrating experience at the ER, I finally saw a gastroenterologist. They sent me home with some collection bottles and instructions on how to collect my poop for them.

I laugh as I tell you this because it was a unique experience, the trouble was that I was out of the house most of the day due to commuting to our new workplaces out of state and only ever had the urge for a bowel movement while I was at work. Awkward is certainly a way to describe this unique collection adventure.

Upon submitting my collections, I became more nervous and a bit hopeful that I would finally get an answer to why I felt so terrible and had to continually suffer with these cramping episodes. The call I got from the doctor was of disbelief, confusion, and a bit of that hope I was banking on. The doctor called me to tell me that I had C-Diff which is short for Clostridium difficile infection, one of the most contagious, difficult to manage, and difficult to get rid of spore infection superbugs you could contract. It's usually called the "old person's disease" because many elderly people contract it while in the hospital being treated with antibiotics for some other issue. It is passed through the feces, no matter how small of an amount, that is left on unwashed hands or articles of clothing contaminated after using the bathroom.

So how did I get it then? I worked with people with disabilities about a year before my surgery and if you think about how their health is managed, it is pretty similar to how the elderly are managed, in and out of hospitals, different rounds of antibiotics, not always able to communicate their feelings of sickness, and also the existing issues with physical cleanliness. So, the C-Diff probably laid latent in my gut for a year without me even knowing it was there. This can happen due to the fact that your normal gut flora (the necessary bacteria in your gut that occurs naturally) keeps the infection in check or technically inactive. The antibiotic is the final piece of the puzzle that caused the infection to run rampant in my system and caused so much pain and so many issues. Mom and I were in disbelief when I called her, neither of us could believe the diagnosis at first, but I finally had an answer.

It was at this point, after all the fighting for my sanity and just hoping to be free of the pain, I truly felt God's presence come upon me and bring me peace and comfort I had never known before. It was this peace and comfort that carried me through the hardest parts of my recovery, I just can't believe it even to this day how relentless His gift of love to me was during this very trying time. I was able to persist with a diligence that I would be healed of this monstrosity of a sickness and finally be able to get my health back.

I proceeded to follow the doctor's instructions to get the medicine I needed to start the healing process and ended up having to cut my diet to meat, gluten-free carbs, and fruit.

I honestly couldn't handle any other foods, vegetables were too hard for my gut to process through (vegetables take a good while to digest and my gut found it too exhausting, same with beans as well).

The first round of antibiotics for C-Diff is Flagyl, which doesn't fully kill off the C-Diff anymore due to the fact that C-Diff has built a resistance to this drug but, is the first step of the protocol for treatment so I followed along. C-Diff is a spore so very specific antibiotics are needed to treat this infection; typical antibiotics just allow the C-Diff to grow worse and were the reason it became active in the first place. It did make me feel better because it decreased the amount of the infection, but three to four weeks after starting Flagyl, I tested positive again.

You have to wait about two weeks after completing the round of antibiotics before retesting to allow the cultures to grow back enough and give a proper positive result to see if the infection was still present.

It was then that they put me on the serious antibiotic Vancomycin, which is the same antibiotic that is used to treat MRSA. This drug is so expensive that without insurance, one bottle can cost $1,000. Praise God my insurance dropped it to $10 out of pocket cost for me. I ended up having to have my treatment extended almost an extra week due to the fact that once I started the Vancomycin, I felt my C-Diff symptoms coming back. So, I was already on a tough drug that had to be tapered (it's so tough that you have to work your way up and your way back down from maximum dosage) and now had to take it for a longer amount of time with the effects of it wearing on my body, along with trying to survive every day like I had for months now.

I was so exhausted that I felt like a sleepy cartoon character dragging its arms across the floor because it was so exhausting. I also woke up every morning wanting to punch my fist through the wall. I was just so angry, and this is just because of the effect of C-Diff and my recovery from it with the antibiotics. I couldn't eat the way I wanted, smells were my enemy causing all kinds of nausea, and I had no energy no matter how long I sleep. Sometimes I felt worse waking up than I did going to sleep. If I ate something that didn't agree with me, to spare myself from hours and hours of pain, I concluded that I would have to just throw It up instead. Now I am not bulimic.

I was desperately trying to eat well and eat what my body could handle. Sometimes, though, my food would contain something that I couldn't eat, like gluten, dairy, or eggs, but I wouldn't realize it until my cramping episode would begin and my heart would drop to the floor in horror of what pain was yet to come.

It was like being pregnant, but I didn't even get the joy of having a baby at the end of everything, just my beaten-up body, worn from infection and the treatment of the infection with the task of climbing out of the deep hole I felt like I had been thrown into. Even now I can hardly believe that I am even remotely sane after all of this, but that is our God for you, making us stronger with each battle we face.

During this time of my second round of antibiotics (still the Vancomycin that I was just put on), we were packing and moving out of state, my sister was getting married and I was in charge of the bridal shower. Needless to say, I had a lot going on, but God provided family to help us pack boxes and the other bridesmaids to help make the shower happen. I couldn't do much due to my lack of energy, but Mom and Dad came over on two different occasions where I cooked a dinner I couldn't even eat (I just think the irony of it is funny) and they packed boxes while I brought items over to them to pack up. It's amazing how much you can accomplish like this even while I was still only a shell of my original self in many ways. We moved successfully and the bridal shower was amazing and beautiful.

My only worry now was if my prayer would be answered that I would be tested for C-Diff one last time and that it would come back negative in time for my sister's wedding in late October. If that didn't happen, the next step in my treatment of C-Diff if the test came back positive would be what is called a fecal transplant. This is where they would empty me of my own feces and then place feces from a healthy donor (who knew healthy donors existed for that) into my system to help reset it. Within the healthy feces would contain different additives to help prompt healthy bacteria growth like prebiotics and such to ensure the success of my body finally being rid of C-Diff. Now obviously this can be pretty invasive, mentally and emotionally, but not surgically speaking because the procedure didn't involve going under a knife because who would understand the mechanics and the science behind it. I know that it would have probably been very successful, but the thought of it was quite stressful at the time when all of the other happenings in my life were added on to my overfilled plate.

The big reveal, what happened next? I finally got the call back from the doctor that my last test had brought back the result of "negative"!

My prayers were answered!! I didn't quite believe it when I first heard it, was it finally out? Am I on the path to true healing now? Is the test just a lie or a mistake? I should clarify now what the testing of negative of C-Diff means. Negative does not mean gone or completely killed, it means that it is no longer actively producing and becoming stronger. Could I be completely healed of C-Diff?

Yes, but there is no test for that, that is God's decision that a human can't clarify with current technology. Like I said before, C-Diff can lay latent in your system while your gut flora keeps it contained. So, what does that mean for me in the future? Any time that I am told that I need to get on an antibiotic, I have to specifically tell them that I have had C-Diff and cannot use typical antibiotics. I did have to take an antibiotic the winter right after being 'cleared' of C-Diff due to a lengthy sinus infection that gave me a fever of 103 degrees for three days.

I was put on Doxycycline which is an antibiotic that is very hard on your gut health (a friend of mine has long term issues now due to Doxycycline). I was discouraged after completing that antibiotic because I felt like I had taken one step forward and four steps back. Fear still grips me any time I think about possibly needing an antibiotic because I never want to feel this sick ever again.

I kept pushing forward though. I knew one day I would be able to surpass the person I wanted to be and become even greater than who I was before I was sick, and I am stronger now because of this experience!

It has now been over a year and seven months since my diagnosis and over a year and five months since receiving the results of my last test. I am finally back to the person I knew I could be and working towards the person I want to be. I am no longer a shell of myself like when I was sick!

I am vibrant again, full of life, and finally able to feel a passionate love that I had forgotten about even after my negative test results. I have felt like I can truly see my husband again, and I mean a 'see' that is beyond his presence but is in admiration and longing that this sickness stole from me for too long. I start to tear up as I write this because I know how hard he worked to help me reach this point in my life where I can finally flourish and be happy with who I am and where I am going. He stood by my side, by the grace of God, and persisted with me in this journey even though he lost the woman he married for many months on end. It truly broke his heart and our family's heart to see me lose myself in this sickness as I just tried to survive every day, to keep pushing for the next day to come, to keep fighting for myself. Despite the pain, anxiety, anger, and disappointment, my husband has stood by my side through it all.

As the tears keep rolling down my face, I can't tell you enough how much this man means to us. Through blood, sweat, and tears, he will truly love you and show you what it truly means to be loved as one loves himself and as our Almighty and Unrelenting God loves and pursues us.

Though the recovery has been long, strenuous, and emotional, I praise God because I am now on the other side of this.

I still have to watch what I eat intently, but the cramping episodes are now fewer and farther between. I know that one day I will be completely healed of all of the repercussions of this process on my body. Another blessing in the midst of the valley is that God has placed His hands on our family and is allowing us the honor of bearing a child. The first trimester was very rough with experiencing very similar symptoms as C-Diff and struggling to believe that it's not the C-Diff for almost two months. I had a lot of emotional junk to work through in trusting God through this. I asked God many times, "Why do I have to go through this again? Why do I have to suffer like this again? I just want to heal and be free!"

I realized that even though I grieved over the trauma of what happened at the one-year anniversary of the first being diagnosed with C-Diff, I hadn't truly let it go in every aspect of my being. I felt like I wasn't allowed to let it go until I didn't have the side effects of all this trauma anymore. Lies! A friend reminded me recently that it all belongs at the foot of the cross, no matter what it is and whether or not you're in the thick of it. As a Christian we have the responsibility to bring it to the cross first and just leave it there for God to do His will with us and the situations we experience. I wish I had realized this when I was struggling to let go of the baggage of C-Diff while in my first trimester. It would be so much easier for me to rejoice in this pregnancy now that I am feeling healthier and freer in my second trimester and to better able to realize the blessing of becoming a mother of a child growing inside of me.

I wish I could give you this letter, younger me, but I am glad that I can't. God brings situations into your life to make you amazing, not to punish you or to completely destroy who you are because His love is beyond your actions and He designed you perfectly to be exactly who you are. God does not cause illness to prove anything. He is simply the peace to get through the journey strengthening us daily.

Growing pains are inevitable though, and obviously, that term can be quite literal. You are a work in progress, never to end up half-baked or unfinished but to be slowly nurtured, masterfully crafted, pressed and stretched, and to be made stronger when broken. However, God sees us as a finished work.

Despite what has happened and the fact that I still have a lot of healing to be done in me, I wouldn't change it.

I am by no means saying that I want to relive it, but I like who I am becoming because of what you will soon go through. And now we get to be a mom like we always wanted, taking on a lifelong challenge helping to raise God's children up in His Word and love with the most amazing man we could have never dreamed up.

I have begun to thank God for you because so often I resent where I have come from, but you are beautiful and amazing. I am glad to have known you, honored to know who we are now, and excited to meet who we will be.

I can now allow God to bring in a peace I wouldn't let you have for a long time, I let you stay angry and hurt and damaged for too long, and I can now lay to rest you and who you will become after this mess. I can now remember you with joyful understanding and with a peaceful presence knowing that I went through this for a reason, and not just for me but to help someone else to not lose hope. I might not see the big picture yet, but I can now accept that God is one with me, He is a big piece in my healing, not forgotten or left in the shadows, but vibrantly depicted with His joy consuming me.

So long, my dear friend, you have been well kept in the presence of God and I praise Him for all that He has done and will do in and through you.

Love,

Yourself

Thank you, my dear sweet friend, for sharing openly the intricate details of the illness, the struggle emotionally, and the hope you have experienced in your personal journey. Congratulations on the birth of your beautiful baby. Your faith is so encouraging.

Addiction

No parent ever looks at their little baby and imagines that their child will become an addict. I know I never imagined that my dad would use drugs. I mean, growing up he was a very strict dad. He would say, "If I ever catch you using drugs, I'll shove them down your throat," along with other threats.

I remember one evening my brother told me to look out my window from the second floor at our dad still sitting in the car. He said, "Dad's smoking weed." I didn't believe him. Dad smoked cigars, pipes, and cigarettes, but not weed, at least that's what I thought. Was he experimenting? I don't know. I certainly knew better than to ask him. I was about thirteen years old and I had enough problems with the abuse not to "stir the pot" and make him angry.

Some years later when I was engaged to my now ex-husband, I received a phone call from dad just five days before the wedding. Dad asked if he could borrow some money. I said that I just did the grocery shopping and paid the bills. I didn't have any money left. Everything else was tied up in the wedding. He said he really needed the money for something to eat. I said I just made shepherd's pie and I can drive the forty-five minutes to his place and bring him some. He said, "That's okay, honey, never mind," and he hung up the phone.

The following night, my brother called me and said that I needed to go see dad. He didn't give me much information, just told me where to go. I pulled up to a facility still ignorant of what was going on. I approached the lady at the front desk and said I was here to visit my dad and gave her his name. I signed a book, gave my license, emptied the contents of my purse, and was frisked. I was given a badge and followed someone back to what I thought would be a hospital room. I was surprised, to say the least, about having to empty my purse and especially the frisking.

It wasn't a hospital. It was a "common area" and I was asked to have a seat. My dad came out of a room wearing a robe and slippers. He looked horrible. He was shaking and stuttering and looking around a lot. He asked if I knew what was going on. I said, "No." In my mind, I thought he had an illness or medical condition. He had a stroke before, so I thought this might have something to do with it.

We were called into the room that he had come out of when I arrived. The person in the room asked dad and me to sit down after introducing themselves to me. They asked me if I knew why I was there. I got a little angry and said, "No, I'm not being told anything, and people keep asking me the same thing."

I said, "Dad, are you all right?" With tears in his eyes, he was shaking and stuttering.

The other person said to dad, "Why don't you tell your daughter what's going on?"

Dad proceeded to tell me that he was a heroin user and that the money he was going to give me to pay for the wedding reception, he already used. Also, when he called for money, it was because he needed a fix. He cried and said he was sorry. I was in shock. To be honest, I had no idea he was doing heroin. He also shared he was at this facility to get help, that he had also tried to hang himself in desperation. He was hurting.

Would it resolve anything for me to lash out at him? No. I accepted his apology and said I would help in any way I could. However, I would never give him cash in the future.

Some time passed and dad had been released from the facility. I was visiting during Christmas and in his kitchen, I happened upon a vial and other drug paraphernalia on his counter. I left. I don't even remember what I said to him at that point. We didn't talk for a few years after that. He wasn't much for keeping up with birthdays, even though my birthday was only one day before his then second wife's birthday.

Years later dad came to visit me in Pennsylvania. I didn't know it at the time, but he was still using. That was December of 1996. While he was staying with us, his tooth was impacted, and Christmas Eve I took him to the dentist who pulled his tooth while I held his hand. After Christmas, dad returned to Massachusetts and I ended my marriage to my husband and got my own apartment.

A couple of months later, dad contacted me looking for help. He said he hated to admit it, but he was pretty much destitute, sick, and practically homeless. He was crying on the phone. I learned a long time ago to never give money to him. I took the number he gave me and said I will call some people in Massachusetts and see if I can get him some help. I called mom. She and her fiancé had a home with a vacant second-floor apartment. They took him in and got him some help, meth treatments at the VA. Years later, dad was diagnosed with Hep C and suffered for years physically from this. What happened to him was out of some sort of nightmare resulting in his death from Stage 4 liver disease.

Addiction takes lives, ruins lives, breaks up families, ruins health, costs money and integrity. If you or someone you know battle with addiction, please take the first step: Admit it, then ask for help. You don't have to go through this alone. God loves you and has a plan and a purpose for your life.

"For I know the plans and thoughts that I have for you," *says the Lord, "plans for peace and well-being and not for disaster, to give you a future and a hope."*

Jeremiah 29:11 (AMP)

The thief comes only in order to steal and kill and destroy. I came that they may have and enjoy life, and have it in abundance [to the full, till it overflows].

John 10:10 (AMP)

An enemy of your soul is addiction. Addiction wants you broken. Jesus is life and life more abundant.

What might seem like a quick fix promises to be a lifestyle of suffering. Don't suffer alone, reach out and take back your life.

There is a national hotline in the back of this book to contact for help.

In this next chapter, a young lady who soon became a dear friend does not pull any punches and shares her testimony, the struggles, the losses, the deals, imprisonment, recovery, and hope. Thank you, sweetness, for sharing the battle that almost took everything from you. I'm so proud of you. Love ya, girl.

Addiction, Violence, Recovery, & a Little Girl's Prayer

I connected with this incredible woman through a mutual friend. We sat at my dining room table as she shared her story with me. She truly has a desire to help others who are battling addiction. Addiction tried to rob her of her life, her family, and her freedom. However, greater is He who is in us than He who is in the world. As you read about her testimony, I hope you do so with an open heart and one of understanding. You are not your past, but through Christ, all things are made new.

My family dynamics: I have an older sister, different dads, never mattered, we were half-sisters in the family sense. Our dads were different people. My dad played a role in my addiction. He was an alcoholic, sold drugs, cocaine probably after being discharged from the military. He never went to rehab, but would be clean periodically, looking back on it now he may have had PTSD.

He was a hard worker, raised in farm life until military. He was introduced to substances on base, partied on weekends. He was active duty for a while, damaged hearing because of I.E.D. explosions, served two years in Germany. After that Army reserves, got a job in steel mill.

His substance abuse caused the separation of my parents. When I was two years old, Mom gave him an ultimatum, either continue the unhealthy lifestyle or leave. He chose to leave.

After the divorce, he picked me up and he would be the "weekend Disneyland dad." He would throw money at me to make up for not being there for me. I remember mom not allowing me to visit with him because he owed child support money. Mom always had a resentment toward my dad, and I felt that trickled down to me.

My sister was a straight "A" student and her dad was completely opposite of my dad. Even though he lived in Texas. He worked with computers back in the '80s. He always sent extra money on top of paying his child support. My mom and both my sister and I's dads all went to high school together. Mom moved fast getting married, having a kid, getting divorced, then marrying my dad, having me, and divorcing my dad.

Mom never battled with addiction. She said she doesn't like the feeling of maybe how drugs make her feel out of control. At one point, I witnessed mom, a single parent raising two daughters, working to provide for us, eventually losing our home and we had to move into the duplex my aunt and uncle owned.

They lived on one side of the duplex and the three of us lived on the other side. We lived there rent free, but mom paid the utilities, so she could get back on her feet. While mom also paid to put herself through nursing school.

I spent a lot of time with my grandparents who lived right down the road. I remember lying in my bed talking to my grandfather who passed, as if he was able to answer. I was scared because my mother was at work and my aunt and uncle lived in the house on the other side of the wall. I'd ask Jesus to tell my pap I loved him and asked if I could talk to him, as if I was calling him on the phone. I'd say things like don't let that noise I just heard be someone coming in the house to get me. Nothing ever happened to me or my sister who was sleeping down the hall.

My pap came over from Italy when he was seven or eight. He spoke Italian. He was a prominent male role model in my life until he died of cancer when I was eight. He was the first person I ever saw suffer a long illness and die. After pap died, my uncle stepped in to be a role model for me. My dad moved to Virginia, so I would go spend summers with him.

I've seen my mom drink a couple of wine coolers at a barbeque. She doesn't even like that. I think she just carries it, so people think she is "having fun." Mom has had surgeries and won't take prescription pain killers because of how they make her feel.

My story of addiction began as I witnessed the lifestyle my dad was living. At a picnic on the 4th of July, I would go get beers from the cooler for people and I would take sips and they thought it was cute. I never really liked alcohol. As I got older, my family made moonshine, and I would go out into the woods and drink it. Dad was an alcoholic and he always had Jim Beam/Pepsi in a big squeeze bottle with a straw walking around drinking. He was a functioning alcoholic. He worked and paid the bills, but was blitzed. He drank so much you could never even tell he was drunk. You could smell it on him though.

I started smoking and I remember being at a party and dad would give me his cup and tell me to go out to the truck and mix him a drink. I would fix it and drink half of it and he would say okay, would you go back and make me one now. He knew I was drinking. He didn't discipline me. I think it was because I was with him. I don't know, that's not really a good excuse. Because dad was an alcoholic and did drugs there were whispers in the family. They couldn't believe my mom let me go stay with him during the summers.

I found my dad's stash of cocaine and weed. I put it back. I didn't try it. I did end up selling weed when I was older though. I remember those whispers about dad and recalling how his friends would come over and he would send me on a bike ride, and when I got back, he would say, "That wasn't long enough." They were smoking weed. I would find rolled up dollar bills never realizing back then he was snorting coke. All these things started clicking into place. I thought, "Oh my god. My dad is the person all these people said he was." That didn't really change anything, just that I knew his secret.

Dad would take me to a game and send me to the concession stand with a $100 bill. The people at the stand would look at me like I was nuts because the hot dog was about 75 cents. I would pocket the money and bum 75 cents off someone else. He would give me his credit card to go to the mall, and I would come back with nothing. He would say, "You mean you couldn't find anything at the mall?" That's not what I wanted. I just wanted to spend time with him. I ended up getting hooked up with one of his pot dealers and I started selling weed. This old hippie dude never told dad.

I started smoking weed when I was sixteen. I had a job at fourteen, so I would flip my own money to deal weed. When dad found out I smoked cigarettes, he made me smoke a whole pack of Lucky Strikes, one right after another. I got up and threw up. I was like, "Oh, my God, I need a Marlboro."

Dad shook his head and said, "Your mother is going to kill me." He told my mom and she was the one who told him to punish me that way. I used to take cigs from my aunt who lived next door and she never knew because she would buy a carton and dump them in a big bowl on the top of her fridge never really knowing that I was taking them. I was about fourteen or fifteen when I started smoking cigs. I would then sell the cigs I would steal from my aunt.

I liked smoking weed and I would go to parties and try anything. If I didn't like it, I wouldn't do it again. I tried crack, didn't like it. I used coke at parties. I used crystal meth for two years while I was in high school.

My mom had no clue. She thought I was getting up when she got home after working a 7pm to 7 am shift. Actually, I hadn't slept in days. I was getting good grades and still working. It was free because I was helping and not getting caught. Some I would sell and some I would keep and use. After two years of this lifestyle, I started getting bad headaches. I stayed up for sixteen days in a row sleep deprived. I finally fell asleep sitting up for 72 hours. I don't know how I didn't die. I didn't eat for those 72 hours nor did I use the bathroom.

When I got into nursing, I found out people can die of dehydration in three days. I got migraines and just stopped using the meth after that episode. I never really liked anything that kept me up after that. I got into downers and pain pills after my wisdom teeth were pulled. I tried morphine sulphate MS-Contin. Then after high school, I sold heroin because it was popular at the time.

When I was in college, I decided to sell drugs to pay for my education. I got my LPN. I got pregnant at the end of my LPN. I finished my last pack of cigs and quit everything even weed. I was going to go back and get my RN when my son started kindergarten. After nursing school, I hurt my back lifting a patient. I started taking pain pills and got addicted and then started using heroin. I was selling within three months. I was shooting up an insane amount like fifty bags a day within four months. I was on my knees begging to go to rehab.

I was twenty-three and my husband and I were strung out with a newborn. I called my mom. She took care of my son and got me to rehab. I knew I couldn't go back to my husband because he was still using.

In 2000, I got married, got pregnant, and graduated college as an LPN. In 2003, I was losing it all. It started spiraling out of control after the injury and getting hooked on pain pills oxycontin. I tried telling my doctor that I didn't think I was taking them right and he prescribed more of them, so I added the heroin. Suboxone is what they are giving people now who are detoxing down from heroin and it's prescribed as a pain killer by doctors. Heroin is an extremely hard drug to come off of. Back when I was coming off it in rehab, I was sick for seven days and they didn't prescribe suboxone to come down. I couldn't keep anything down. I lost twenty pounds in seven days. I thought it was horrible. I could stay clean and yet I was only clean for four months after that.

I was in and out of rehab. In 2004, I was arrested for a felony charge. I took my mom's card and wired money to myself but told my mom what I did and gave the money back. But later when I was relapsed, my mom contacted the police and that was my felony charge. I was at Walmart stealing a pair of underwear and I ended up going to jail for that. Three days before sentencing, I found out I was pregnant with my daughter.

I was couch surfing mostly living on the streets. I didn't know if I was going to keep her. Her dad was a crack dealer. I was living dirty. I was helping him sell. I had nothing. My mom had my son. I was in and out of jail. I went to sentencing and told the judge I couldn't go to jail because I needed to get an abortion. The judge said it isn't life threatening, so he ended up sentencing me. That pregnancy wound-up helping me get out of jail early.

The lady at the drug and alcohol classes in jail suggested I be forthcoming about the pregnancy. I went to rehab then a halfway house for six months. Then I went to a supportive housing program for women with children. I got my son back to live with me there. I had seven years clean after that.

Then my back pain started up again, I had two surgeries back to back, and the pain meds came into play again. I went to a pain clinic that was sensitive to my situation. I had a pinched nerve. I was getting pain shots and was put on morphine. I was on it for a year. I lost my job and couldn't pay to go to the clinic anymore, so I bought some "Roxy's" (Roxicodone) on the street. I was hooked again. I was shooting up again.

I started a new job when I turned thirty. I got a new house and a car. I was living near my mom with my two kids until this last relapse. I got involved with some "out of state" guys. Now I'm living off Social Security from my husband's death. We were separated when he died. I'm back on heroin and selling it. I was showing these guys around the area. $60 a gram there and I could sell it for more than three times that amount. They wanted to use my house and me as a front because I was an urban housewife with kids. No one was coming to my house to buy drugs.

Occasionally, these dudes would come get more "stuff," and drop some money off. I had so much money stashed in my house. I got arrested for that driving back from "out of state" with drugs in the car. I lost my home.

My son turned thirteen while I was in jail. He went to live with his other grandma and my daughter went to live with my mom. Their life was ruined, no house, friends gone. They put the puzzles to our life together. I get out of jail, start getting my life back together, get an apartment, etc. Then one of "those guys" gets out of jail and moves in two doors down from me.

I'm like, "Oh my God. Here's the devil." Before you know it, he's always coming over and I'm selling again. I just got out of jail, by the grace of God. I should have done eight years. I'm thinking if I use again, it's like I'm kicking God in the teeth. He's gotten me out of so much. I mean, I should have been dead by some of the situations I got myself in.

I start using, my kids don't want to live with me. Even the dealers don't want anything to do with me. I think I am okay, but I am not. Things go crazy, shootings are happening, my kid is holding a gun. Dealers are on the floor; cops didn't know I had forty grams of heroin in my bra.

Cops came to tell me my gas meter got shot in a drive by. They didn't know the dealers were in my house who were being shot at.

I go to my neighbor's house and I watched everyone leave out of my house. I had been living right across from a magistrate office, so there were videos of what had been going on.

Ten days later I'm now living with some girl after the cops raided the apartment at 9 am. They are looking for the "out of state guy" who left at midnight. They didn't have the right address on the warrant because I had moved. I don't get arrested because to them I'm just a junky. I would be a burden on society. So, I'm homeless and dope sick because all the dealers left town. Now they surround my car while I'm trying to buy. They still won't arrest me. I'm practically begging to be arrested because to me they are destroying my life. At least if I was arrested, I would get something to detox. Now I'm staying with someone else and babysitting during the day. So that I wouldn't get sick, her baby's dad would give me a bag.

One night while I'm lying on this guy's couch, I realize I'm homeless and I can't get into rehab. I haven't talked to my mom in months. I'm lying there and I'm like, "Oh, my God, you got to help me get out of this." I realized I wasn't even living. I was praying because now this guy was trying to proposition me. I was scared.

The very next day, these people come around with flyers for a church. I would normally tell people I'm an atheist even though I'm Christian because they don't know what to say and usually just leave me alone at that point. But the lady said something about taking prayers or something and I thought, "Yeah, I need you to pray for me." I thought they were just going to write my name down. They ended up coming into this guy's house I was at while he was at work.

This lady began talking to me about everything I was feeling inside and I began tearing up. She held my hands and she said her prayers. The next day was mom's birthday. I hadn't talked to her in months. I texted her, "Happy Birthday." She texted back, "Where are you?" I happened to be a few miles up the road. I ended up going to her house.

There it was, my bank statement with proof of address and proof of income. The two things I needed to get funded to go to county rehab, sitting on her counter. Mom and I talked and she picked me up the next day. I stayed with my mom until Friday when I went to fill out paperwork to go to the county rehab.

They could get me in, but not for three days. Mom let me stay with her. It was rough. I had it rough, so my mom helped me through it.

God answered my prayers. I ended up getting funded for ninety days. I would eventually move to where I'm at now while my mom watched my daughter. Although my son still wasn't talking to me.

I was moving here to be in a program that would be a seven-month-long program. I needed that. While going through recovery, I had no reason to turn to drugs and do what I did. My sister went through the death of her child and even she didn't turn to drugs. Because of my "religious" upbringing, my dad stopped drinking at some point in my life and was born again; he became a "bible thumper." I was raised when I was young in the Catholic church. Mom was excommunicated from the Catholic church because of divorce, so mom started going to a Presbyterian church.

Grandma was a devout Catholic. I used to go to mass with grandma on Saturday nights. Because she served communion wine on Sunday morning, I would go with mom to Presbyterian church. When I was about seventeen, I said, "Screw it all." I didn't want any of it. The religious stuff pushed me away from going to church. I read the Bible; I prayed. I talked with God "like he's my homeboy." He's always been there for me, but I never found the right church.

For anyone who is where I was, pay attention to that small voice inside you that offers hope, that there is a better life out there. I no longer have the desire to use, and that itself is a miracle.

Go through the programs; stick it out. It is possible to be a productive member of society. I know that now. I needed that day of praying for a change in my life because I felt soulless, unrecognizable—even to myself. That prayer I prayed on that man's couch changed everything.

No matter if I was a little girl praying scared in my bed, praying in my jail cell, praying while being shot at, or praying to get off that man's couch, God has answered my prayers in one way or another, according to His plan.

Whatever part I am to play in God's plan must be big and I'm ready for whatever He has for me.

Anxiety and Depression

Two different words, yet one outcome. They both can debilitate the individual who is dealing with one or the other or perhaps both. As far back as I can remember, I struggled with anxiety and depression to the point I became fearful. I heard people say, "Oh, she's just shy."

You see, my dad and mom would fight. I could hear what was said and I would get very anxious to the point I had severe stomach problems. I would be thinking very dark thoughts for a little girl. I would get so depressed that I would become extremely emotional and break down into tears. As I got older, I never really dealt with this. I just suppressed it.

My friend's mom, as thoughtful as she thought she was being, gave me very poor advice. She said, "Just put it on a shelf and never dust it." I tried that. It didn't work because there are some things we just carry around like luggage. Sometimes this would contribute to my already low self-esteem. I found it very difficult to advocate for myself and speak up.

As I got older and life's storms came, I dealt with anxiety and depression by staying in bed and taking the highest doses of anti-depressants the doctor would prescribe. Pardon the analogy, but that was like putting a band-aid on a severed limb. I wasn't getting better. I was just numbing the past as well as the present. I tried going to therapy and support groups, but never got to the core of where this stemmed from. It was time to go to that "shelf" and dust the pain from the past. I needed to confront the enemy of my past pains face to face. I need to combat them with the Word of God. I need to decree what God has already said about me in Christ Jesus.

And my God will liberally supply (fill until full) your every need according to His riches in glory in Christ Jesus.
Philippians 4:19 (AMP)

And the peace of God [that peace which reassures the heart, that peace] which transcends all understanding, [that peace which] stands guard over your hearts and your minds in Christ Jesus [is yours].
Philippians 4:7 (AMP)

In studying the scriptures, I became aware of who I needed to rely on, where I could find comfort and not be let down. People and things are flawed, even under the best intentions or conditions.

It has been my experience that the more I searched the scriptures the more I found out that as I revealed these pains, thoughts, emotions, and past abuses that I was comforted by the compassion I found only in Christ Jesus.

> *Blessed [gratefully praised and adored] be the God and Father of our Lord Jesus Christ, the Father of mercies and the God of all comfort, who comforts and encourages us in every trouble so that we will be able to comfort and encourage those who are in any kind of trouble, with the comfort with which we ourselves are comforted by God.*
>
> 2 Corinthians 1:3-4 (AMP)

Now mind you, this was a process for me. Like I said, before that, I had to trust. I had to renew my mind so that a transformation could take place. Before I knew it, I thought differently about the past hurts, abuse, self-loathing, doubts, and fears. I was no longer lying in bed or on the sofa with curtains drawn for days.

I was no longer relying on high doses of anti-depressants, which by the way for me had tremendous side effects. I found a renewed strength in Christ Jesus, a renewing of my spirit and flesh. I wake up now eager to spend time with God in His Word studying and starting my day with His promises and hope. Hope in the scripture means a strong and confident expectation.

So prepare your minds for action, be completely sober [in spirit—steadfast, self-disciplined, spiritually and morally alert], fix your hope completely on the grace [of God] that is coming to you when Jesus Christ is revealed.

1 Peter 1:13 (AMP)

May the God of hope fill you with all joy and peace in believing [through the experience of your faith] that by the power of the Holy Spirit you will abound in hope and overflow with confidence in His promises.

Romans 15:13 (AMP)

In my journey of healing, I encountered a woman and became friends with a woman who has overcome anxiety and depression. In this next chapter may her story of healing encourage you.

Love ya lady.

A Daughter's Anxiety and Depression

As the youngest child and only daughter of three children to two ministers, my life was like living in a fishbowl. Literally, a large extended family that included one hundred and five cousins while living in a small city, there was always someone to report back to my parents any misconduct from my brothers and me. I truly felt like I had to play the part as a minster's child—always be on my best behavior and smile big. I was a naturally shy, gullible girl, and I quickly gained the affection of many of the mothers in my church.

I would often hear conversations my mom would have after Sunday morning service, as I was glued to her hip and another mother would say, "I pray I have a daughter like yours!" I truly lost sight of who I was. Depression set in and I became a loner. I didn't understand then the calling on my life, how God's hand and grace covered me, and others could see and respect that. I stood-out but felt like I just wanted to be normal. My friends and family that weren't believers didn't use profanity or vulgar language around me. I just wanted to be treated like everyone else.

As my parents continued to attempt to instill in my brothers and me a Godly foundation and create an atmosphere not filled with drunken fights like they experienced in their childhoods, an atmosphere of peace with both parents present. This was because if we weren't in church, we were having church at home! I'm talking full worship, Bible reading, and prayer! My friends knew if they stayed the night, we were having church. Later I found out our worship sessions could be heard outside banging tambourines, clapping, and singing. Although I am grateful now for my foundation, I heard repeatedly the stories of Noah building the Ark, Jonah in the belly of the whale, and the birth of Jesus. I became numb to the faith that brought these testimonies to fruition.

Even though I lost sight of who I was in Christ, I truly thought everyone in the world was a Christian and they all believed in the Bible. As I said, I was gullible and quickly learned as a teenager how cruel people could be. When I turned eleven, all that I knew to be true now felt like a lie. My parents sat my brothers and me down at the dining room table for a talk. With hesitance and a heavy heart, my mother told us my dad committed adultery and she wanted us to hear it from them and not by someone else, mainly because my dad got fired from his job for his actions. The darkness of depression quickly set in as I attempted to process and understand what I was just told. I couldn't respond.

I just got up from the table, put a leash on my dog, and walked for what seemed like hours. It was late in the evening and the sun had already gone down.

My mind was a whirlwind of questions and my anxiety went into full throttle. What did we do to deserve this? Why wasn't my mom enough? I couldn't even look my dad in the eyes the next few days; he just disgusted me. I began to have sleepless nights. I often just sat in my room lost and gazing out the window daydreaming of the life I thought I was supposed to have.

In this time of darkness with depression, I began writing poetry and it was always about pain and hurt. Along with the gloomy writing, I would have visions about women being abused or raped. The visions became reality on the local news. I began crying out to God as to why I was given these visions and although I prayed against the harm, it didn't stop, and the bad news continued. As the questions continued to circle in my head, for years there were no answers to reassure me things would get better. However, I maintained my personal relationship with God. He was my true friend and I would spend time daily as I lay in my bed just talking to Him about my day and laughing about funny moments.

This was my only comfort and place of peace for the time being. As I watched my mother remain the Proverbs 31 woman, she never raised her voice to my dad or demeaned him. I begged her to divorce him. I felt her pain. Seeing her like this caused a deep anger to brew within me that I couldn't control.

I was always taught, "abstinence until marriage." But why? So I could just be cheated on? Absolutely not. I'm not going to my husband a virgin. I grew a hate for men and believed they were all the same. I decided I would lose my virginity, and I did just that when I turned seventeen. A guy whom I was introduced to and who claimed to be a Christian also.

However, within a year I felt guilt and shame and broke off the relationship and told him I needed to get my life back on track with God. I dove head in. I went with a group called "Teen Maria" on a mission trip to impoverished areas of Mexico. I felt at home witnessing to the little town about the good news of Christ. I witnessed a demon-possessed man set free; it was awesome. They realized the true power of God!

However, a year after I returned home from my week-long mission trip, my grandmother died due to complications with diabetes. I was very close to her and would spend countless hours with her just talking. I adored her and was completely devastated by her death.

She was my bridge connecting me with my aunts and uncles and cousins. Without her, I was an outcast. She was my gem, my home away from home. She always encouraged me to do good. I'd never had anyone close to me pass away and I spiraled out of control.

I found friends to carry out my mourning with, friends who wouldn't tell me to just pray about it. Instead, we numbed it with beer and alcohol. I spiraled out of control, I began drinking and became promiscuous. When I was sober, anxiety and depression convinced me I wasn't good enough, now I'm tainted, and I've failed everyone. My consolation, more drinking which lead to poor decisions and endless nights crying, wanting to erase the past.

I became a mother at the age of twenty-four and felt like I was lost in the desert. I didn't know who I was or the plans for my life, now I have a son to raise?

The drinking was my only comfort. I reached a point where nothing was working out. I attempted to go to a community college near me, but as life's obstacles tripped me up, I quit classes. I worked in various job categories, but wasn't satisfied. I finally found comfort in helping others in the medical field. As my experience matured, my love life declined.

I wore my father's infidelity on my sleeve as a right to not trust men and the reason for my sadness and pain. Each relationship I went into I played the victim and shared my pain. By the time my son was five, I had enough. I needed to get away and start new.

I had a friend in New Jersey who had been wanting me to move with her, so I made the bold move to do so. Without a job, I packed my car and left Pennsylvania. God opened a door and I was employed by the main hospital in southern Jersey, and he didn't stop there. I found an apartment six walking blocks from the beach! It was heaven on earth for my son and me! I had such peace in the time I lived there, it was a year of rejuvenation! However, it ended when my son became homesick. It was a three-hour drive back to Pennsylvania, but his visits didn't suffice, so we moved back to Pennsylvania. I felt like I failed and walked with my tail between my legs, like a bad dog.

A year later, God revealed to me the answer to my prayers regarding the women in my visions. My friend Lisa was involved with a women's ministry for domestic violence victims. I immediately felt God lead me to talk with her to find out how I could help.

As time progressed, I began to learn the steps to bring a woman to safety that is in need. God began showing me how to heal with my pain from my dad's betrayal. Soon after God spoke to me and said, "It's time for you to stop playing the victim and take responsibility for your wrong choices." I surrendered to God and understood that bad things will happen in life, but God is my strength and will never leave me.

As I looked back on the times where everyone else turned their backs on me, I noticed God always received me with open arms. His love never changed, it stayed the same. I felt brand new, armed with a confidence that I never had.

I continue to be faithful and trusted God for a husband. A prophet visited my church and she asked all the single people to come to the front for prayer if they were trusting God for a mate. When it was my turn, she spoke over me and said, "You have a spirit like a dove. When you meet your husband, you won't have to fight," something I was used to because I felt like I didn't deserve better. Although I felt changed, I still had negative thoughts towards my dad.

I went to my pastor and expressed my concern. I didn't understand why although I prayed for forgiveness, I still held anger towards him. I was advised to write my dad a letter detailing my feelings and expressing that I forgave him.

It took me three weeks to muster up the courage to even begin writing. Once I finished the letter and placed it in the mailbox (because I couldn't hand-deliver it, even though we lived in the same city), the instant that I dropped the envelope in the box, I felt a huge weight off my chest. I was finally free from anxiety, depression, shame, and guilt. The sky seemed bluer and life finally felt right!

Within a few months, I was reunited with a man I was introduced to while I lived in New Jersey, but I didn't let him get close to me because I thought he'd be like every other guy I met.

He knew what he wanted and within six months, we were engaged. As I held onto the word spoken in my life, I stood in amazement of how good God was. He continued to take the lead and prove he was for me. I didn't have to pull or fight for his affection. We were married five months later in a quiet ceremony in my pastor's office due to his working on the road, and now we are having a honeymoon baby.

Words cannot express how good God has been in delivering me from my past. I'm not looking back, no longer the lost girl who was hopeless. Now I'm walking out God's plan for my life and holding my head high, for there is no greater joy! My husband encouraged me to go back to school – my heart's desire.

I was going to change my major from nursing to social work because math is my weak subject, but he wouldn't let me settle for less than what I wanted.

Self-Harm

This chapter is a very painful subject, a very real one for many who continue to battle in darkness. Self-harm, also known as self-injury or self-mutilation, has been described as a coping mechanism. Self-harm includes the cutting of oneself but goes far beyond that to any action a person can use to purposely harm oneself. Here are but a few: self-injuries are most commonly inflicted on the arms, hands, and wrists of the individual but other body parts such as thighs, stomach, and back have also been reported as self-mutilation sites.

Eating disorders: addiction behaviors are not typically considered methods of self-harm, but in some cases, they may be if the intent of their use is to cause harm to the body. Now that is how the medical community views this torment.

Along my journey of healing, I have come to a huge revelation. I did not like myself. I certainly did not love myself. If I did not like or love myself, how was I going to like or love others, a spouse, children, etc., thus continuing the path of self-destruction?

The first examples of what a person thinks of themselves for me had to go as far back as to look at the relationship my parents had. Not to put blame on them, but for me, this is where I first remember the "importance" of body image. My dad would "check out" other women and comment on their appearance right in front of my mom. Mom already had and carried a poor self-image because of past abuse so if she already felt "inadequate," then how was she supposed to walk in the confidence of who she was created to be? Let alone guide her daughter in the importance of who she was created to be?

So God created man in His own image, in the image and likeness of God He created him; male and female He created them.

Genesis 1:27 (AMP)

God saw everything that He had made, and behold, it was very good and He validated it completely. And there was evening and there was morning, a sixth day.

Genesis 1:31 (AMP)

There it is, in His own image in the image of God, it was very good. I have always believed in God, yet I didn't understand that because He created me in His image and likeness and that He said I was very good, that should be enough for me. I needed to believe God.

It wasn't because I wanted to please my own flesh. I wanted my dad to tell me I was beautiful. I wanted the boys in school and later in life to swoon over me.

I developed late in life and I remember growing up in a neighborhood that was inhabited by young girls from a different country and pretty much developed at the age of ten and eleven. When I say "developed," I mean they had "boobs" and celebrated their womanhood.

In my bedroom, there was a huge velvet portrait of Jesus wearing the crown of thorns. During prayer one night, I knelt down beside my bed and prayed, "Dear God, can I please have big boobs like my mommy and auntie?" Funny, right? Not to me. I was serious. I thought that if I had big boobs then I would be beautiful. I was a "flat-chested tomboy."

To me, I was not pretty. Wrong. I kept looking at the outside appearance and not my heart. I could not see past that. I remember looking in the mirror on more than one occasion and picking apart every part of my appearance, hair, face, teeth, complexion, weight, clothing.

When I was about thirteen, I began to develop almost overnight. I now weighed just over 100 lbs. I wasn't devastated, just concerned. It must be because I finally have "boobs." I was athletic. I ran like the wind. I was a cheerleader. I could do flips, cartwheels, and splits. I was feeling pretty good about myself. I do recall an argument when my dad screamed to my mom that I was the only reason he even married her. I felt unloved, unwanted, and just plain ugly. Even though he did not say that his words implied it.

There is one who speaks rashly like the thrusts of a sword,
But the tongue of the wise brings healing.

Proverbs 12:18 (AMP)

In the same sense, the tongue is a small part of the body, and yet it boasts of great things. See [by comparison] how great a forest is set on fire by a small spark!

* * *

With it we bless our Lord and Father, and with it we curse men, who have been made in the likeness of God.

James 3:5, 9 (AMP)

Our words have power. It's odd how we will believe the negative someone speaks about us and often put aside the beauty of what God says about us. As I grew into womanhood and in and out of relationships, I was clueless.

At one point I lived at the beach in a bitter relationship and I believed I just couldn't seem to "control" anything that was going on in my life.

In my mind, I could punish myself by limiting my food intake. After all, who cared? I figured I would lose weight and then I would like myself better.

I was on a path of self-destruction: Anorexia. I had lost so much weight, so fast that my clothes draped off of me. I was losing hair by the handful. You could wrap your hands around my waist and your forefingers and thumbs from both hands would meet.

My mother freaked out. She confided to an aunt at a family get together that she was so worried about me. She thought I had cancer. I reassured her I did not. Though, I did have an ulcer from acid eating the stomach lining. A few months later I had moved to Pennsylvania with that abusive spouse.

While in Pennsylvania, the self-punishment continued. If I had to eat around others, I would shift food around on my plate, take a small bite, then when they were not looking, I would spit it into my napkin. I usually covered what was left in the plate with a napkin excusing myself from the table and scraping the plate into the trash.

Sometime later I was in the process of escaping my abuser and trying to figure out how to get out of this nightmare of a marriage. I began self-punishing again denying myself food. I got so bad that I dropped fifteen pounds in one week. I couldn't eat and would gag on toast. I was living on coffee, cigarettes, and pity.

While at work, Ray (Big Daddy) said to me, "Hey. Do you want to go on a delivery with me?" I reluctantly agreed. As we drove down the road, he pulled the truck over and said, "You're probably not going to like this, but you look awful. What's going on?" As almost if to spite him or at least what he said, I just verbally spewed out all that I was dealing with and how I've been looking for a place and I am taking my daughter and moving out. I thought for sure he would think "train wreck" and not want to even speak to me, but that was not the case. He had such compassion in his eyes, not pity, compassion.

I finally got my own place with my daughter and about a month after that I drove up North to visit with my mother in Massachusetts. While at mom's, I took a shower and needed a second towel. I had used the one available to wrap my hair. I cracked open the bathroom door and asked mom to bring one. She came into the bathroom and broke down into tears. She was devastated.

I was a skeleton in the skin. You could count the bones in my spinal cord and rib cage. I won't go into more detail, but you get the picture. The tears in my mother's eyes broke my heart. I came clean about the anorexia. I made a solemn promise that I would not "punish" myself again. That was over twenty years ago. It was not easy. It took some time to heal.

During praise and worship in my office thanking Him for still loving this hot mess (me), He said that's not how I see you.

If this is something that you deal with, please know that even though you may feel alone that you are not. Seek help, physically, emotionally, and spiritually. Talk to a doctor, a nutritionist, pastoral counselor, and talk. Don't travel the road of self-harm alone.

I will give thanks and praise to You, for I am fearfully and wonderfully made; Wonderful are Your works, And my soul knows it very well.

Psalm 139:14 (AMP)

Suicide Attempts

While working in the corporate world, I met a man who entered the office I worked at for a meeting with the president of our company. This man seemed a bit "creepy" to me. After sitting across from me in the waiting area, he went in and met with the president, and when the meeting was over, he left. The president asked me what I thought of the man and I said I thought he seemed "creepy." "Why do you ask? Are you planning on doing business with him and now I'm fired because of my honesty?" He laughed and said, "No, you're not fired," and no, he wasn't going to do business with him. He just thought I could pick up on the way some people behaved and could tell if "they were alright."

Sometime later, not sure how much time had passed, myself and the president were in the office and I was having him sign documents and checks when the phone rang. The call was for him. When he hung up the phone, the look on his face was that of shock and disbelief. I asked him if everything was okay. He re-

minded me of the meeting with the man not long before that. I said I thought was "creepy?" He replied,
"Yes." He then went on to tell me the phone call was
from someone who knew the man and was calling to
tell him the man was at his son's birthday party. When
that man's ex-wife showed up at the party for their son,
he met her in the front yard, shot her, and then killed
himself in front of everyone at the party.

The president and I talked about the situation and
what I said next would come back to disturb me later. I
said, "Wow, you have to be some sort of weak spirit to
commit suicide." To me, I thought he just gave up all
hope.

As I think back on that statement, what an ignorant
and unfeeling thing I said. Perhaps that man's spirit
had been weakened by hardships and whatever else he
had been contending with.

A couple of years later I received a call from my mother that she had stage four cancer. I was three months
pregnant and four states away from mom with a seven-
year-old at home. I would travel back and forth to Massachusetts to help care for my mom. As my belly grew
with this little one developing within me, I watched
feeling helpless as my fifty-six-year-old mom withered
away being ravished by this thief called cancer.

July 24, 2005, surrounded by her loved ones my
mother passed away in my arms. My heart broke. I

cried so hard. This pain of watching her suffer for so many months is indescribable.

After mom passed, I went back to my aunt's house where the family gathered. We were all there to comfort one another. Some were eating and talking.

I decided to go upstairs to take a shower. I had not had a shower in about a week.

I did not leave the hospital room for the last week of mom's life, just giving myself a hobo's bath in the little bathroom sink. I remember standing in the shower and just collapsing under the hot water. I placed my hands over my mouth so that I could scream. My heart was shattered. Later that night I sat in bed looking at my beautiful new baby who was a month old. The thoughts started to rush in. Suicide: I remember thinking, "I can't take the pain. I could do this. I could end my pain." I started planning it. That was July. By August I was finally back in Pennsylvania home with my now eight-year-old, the new baby, and my husband. Still on the highest doses of anti-depressants. I did not tell my husband; as a matter of fact, I didn't tell anyone yet.

I started going back to church in the months that followed. It is now October, just three months after my mom had passed. While I was downstairs helping out in the nursery, a lady from our church came up to me and said that our pastor's wife sent her to talk to me because her husband was just diagnosed with stage four cancer. Are you kidding me? I thought to myself, "I know now that God was already aware of my plan to end my own life." It is obvious to me now that even though it was one of the most horrific times of my life, I was not alone even though it felt that way.

> *God is our refuge and strength [mighty and impenetrable],*
> *A very present and well-proved help in trouble.*
>
> Psalm 46:1 (AMP)

> *Your eyes have seen my unformed substance;*
> *And in Your book were all written*
> *The days that were appointed for me,*
> *When as yet there was not one of them [even taking shape].*
>
> Psalm 139:16 (AMP)

When she came to me to ask for help in what to do next, I couldn't say no. God knew that. I helped coordinate things, so she could still go to work, and people would come and either sit with her husband, cook, and clean, or take him for treatments at the hospital.

I remember sitting in their living room while he slept in the hospital bed. When he would wake up, I would hold the baby up, who was now five months old and he would smile and go back to sleep.

At home one night about two weeks later, I got a phone call from his wife saying that he was not doing well at all and that he was being taken to the hospital. She asked if I could meet them at the ER.

When I arrived, the doctor came in and asked to speak to her outside the room. My heart began to sink. I knew already what he was going to say. I just lived through this a few short months ago with my mom. She asked me to come out into the hall while the doctor spoke to her. The doctor said that all they can do is try to make him as comfortable as possible and that there is not much more that they can do.

As I held her hand, we walked back into the room her husband was in. A relative of theirs arrived and I went home.

I felt numb. My heart ached for her. My own pain of losing my mom was still fresh and the thoughts of ending my life came flooding back. Even though I didn't really know this couple very well, the pain of watching someone else go through what my mom and my family just went through was agonizing. I cried all the way home.

The next day I went to visit at the hospital and told her to call me should she need anything. I was getting ready for bed, had my big baggy jammies on when I got the phone call. She said, "He just passed away." I said, "I am so sorry, sweetie. Is anyone with you?" She said, "Yes," and then she asked me if I could come to the hospital. I put my slippers on, got in the car, and drove there.

As I made my way down the corridor to his hospital room in my jammies, our pastor walked out of the room, saw me coming and said, "Now that's love." He commented that because I apparently looked a mess in my jammies, disheveled hair, and no makeup coming to the room at her request. I gave him a smirk and walked in.

After a couple of minutes in his room, his daughter arrived and when she leaned over to kiss her dad goodbye, I slinked slowly out of the room so as not to make a spectacle of myself.

I was just going to go quietly down the hall, go into the elevator, and leave, but the pastor saw me dip out of the room and grabbed a hold of me and gave me the biggest hug while I literally convulsed in a sea of tears and heartache. I shook so hard if he had not held me with that dad hug, I probably would have hit the floor in a mass of quivering flesh. That was definitely a God hug.

At his celebration of life service, the most beautiful thing happened. His widow danced and worshipped during the praise and worship part of his service. She danced before God and danced for her husband who used to love to watch her praise and worship her King.

I admired her for that. I had seen her in the storm and watched her dance in the puddles. Not because her heart didn't ache, not because she was "performing," but because she truly worshipped God. Even though she was mourning she was celebrating her God who was granting her peace in the midst of her storm.

And the peace of God [that peace which reassures the heart, that peace] which transcends all understanding, [that peace which] stands guard over your hearts and your minds in Christ Jesus [is yours].

Philippians 4:7 (AMP)

Sometime later she said she felt protected and doesn't remember a lot of details, just that she felt covered and loved.

This was December, just five months after mom had passed, and our first Christmas without her. Mom would have been fifty-eight on December 27th. Mom loved Christmas and really celebrated it making sure everyone got a gift and knew that she thought of them, not this year though. She would not be with us physically. I missed her so much.

Now, I am sure that what happened next had to be orchestrated by God. Some will agree and some won't. However, a person with an experience is never at the mercy of a person with an argument.

I was having dark thoughts of suicide. It was getting harder and harder not to feel this way. I kept thinking, "If you only did more, then your mom would not have suffered. It's your fault she died. You should have taken control of her care and made her go to the cancer institute. You're a horrible daughter." These were but a few of the things that the enemy to my soul was bombarding me with. Every time I would close my eyes to sleep, all I could see was my mother emaciated and ravaged by cancer in her petite bedridden frame and not the beautiful vivacious fifty-seven-year-old woman whose smile lit up a room and absolutely loved her family. I was and am sure that just like we can hear God when we just sit and listen that we can also be influenced by dark thoughts as well.

If the enemy to your soul can get you to believe these things, then you will eventually speak these things. For me I was believing I was a horrible daughter, I should have done more, etc. He is the father of lies after all. (Satan, that is.) I was vulnerable and the enemy knew it.

Be sober [well balanced and self-disciplined], be alert and cautious at all times. That enemy of yours, the devil, prowls around like a roaring lion [fiercely hungry], seeking someone to devour.

1 Peter 5:8 (AMP)

I understand it to be God's voice I hear and not the enemy because it will exalt God in the same way it would destroy someone if it is from the enemy.

On a Tuesday night, I decided to go to church. I had everything planned out. I had even begun to write my letter to my family. I was going to do it. I sat about four rows from the back and listened as the pastor spoke. There was something about the atmosphere that was different that night. At the end of the service, the pastor did an altar call. "If you have never confessed Jesus as your Lord and Savior, lift your hand high enough and long enough so we can see it. If you would like us to agree in prayer for healing, please come up so we may pray with you." Pastor said.

I sat there four rows from the back of the church. I didn't budge. I had never gone up for an altar call that I could remember especially for one like this, so I stayed put. Pastor said again to everyone at the service, "if anyone needs prayer, please come up so we can pray with you."

I felt a tap in the back of my head, I looked back and there was no-one close enough to tap me, so I looked forward. Pastor called out for the third time, "The altar is open. If you have a need, don't be shy." "We will gladly agree in prayer whatever your need might be." At that moment, I felt a physical smack in the back of my head. Again, I turned around really quick and there was no one standing close enough to even come close to touching me. So, I said, "All right, all right. I'm going up." Now I don't even know why I said it out loud, but I did.

I headed up to the altar to where the pastor was praying with and over others that walked up before me, with my shattered heart.

The pastor took my hands, leaned forward, and asked me what I needed prayer for. Now up until that time I had only witnessed him pray for someone then give them a hug and they would sometimes fall out in the spirit, but what happened to me next was spiritually aggressive warfare.

I replied to the pastor in a small quiet voice, "I've been having dark thoughts of suicide and I even have a plan." The pastor spoke to that thing and said, "In the name of Jesus, I bind the spirit," and as he continued to help me fight off this attack of the enemy, I began to travail, tears, snot, and I fell to the floor!

I was trembling and crying so hard I was on the floor for what seemed like a long time while three women continued to pray over me.

When I finally stood up a complete physical mess, I was handed some tissues, and the pastor's wife asked if I was okay. She said, "Pastor wants to see you before you go." I walked up to him thinking, "Oh, good. He is probably going to apologize to me," because I was a mess. My clothes and hair were all messed up, my face was puffy from crying so much and everybody saw me. But no, he did not. I said, "Yes, pastor? You wanted to see me again?" And boom. He broke that thing off me in the name of Jesus and down I went again. When I got up this time, I literally felt lighter, as if I wasn't carrying the burden any longer. I was still missing and mourning my mom. I will always miss her. She was my best friend, but now the deep desire to end my life was gone.

When I closed my eyes to go to sleep, I did not see my mom like I did toward the end of her life. I saw her healthy and smiling. Pastor had once said the reason sickness, disease, and death are so hard to bear is because until sin entered in, we were never meant to experience these things. These things were not in the Garden of Eden. As time passed by and with pastoral counseling, I could now enjoy life once again.

If you suffer from thoughts of suicide, please seek help. Talk to your pastor, a counselor, a teacher, or a friend, and please don't suffer in silence.

There is a list of hotlines in the back of this book for help.

Religion Hurt Me

When I was born, it was determined by my family that we were to be raised in the Catholic religion. My dad was brought up Catholic, my mom was brought up Episcopalian. As adults, neither of them was still practicing. They did not attend church when I was a child as far as I knew.

As an adolescent, I observed things that just did not sit right in my spirit. I attended public school and I remember attending Catechism class after school on Tuesdays. I had to go to a parochial school and wait in the basement in the boiler room until their school let out so we could attend these classes to prepare us for our first communion. First communion then allows us as children to receive the Eucharist communion wafer according to Catholicism, not according to Jesus in His Word.

Now as they were eating Jesus took bread, and after blessing it, He broke it and gave it to the dis-

ciples, and said, "Take, eat; this is My body." And when He had taken a cup and given thanks, He gave it to them, saying, "Drink from it, all of you; for this is My blood of the [new and better] covenant, which [ratifies the agreement and] is being poured out for many [as a substitutionary atonement] for the forgiveness of sins."

Matthew 26:26-28 (AMP)

Jesus gave. He did not say you had to go through a "religious ceremony" to receive His body and blood. Before you throw your stones at me, understand me, please. This chapter is about my experiences and how my "Catholic" upbringing in the church I was in almost pushed me away from a relationship with my Creator and Savior. It did not sit right with the spirit that dwelled within me. I was very confused. If Jesus didn't say I had to put on a pretty white dress and go through classes to receive communion, then why? It seemed more like a performance than an inward partnering or rather a remembrance of a memorial unto God for His sacrifices.

After our first communion, on Sunday mornings my brother and I would attend church by ourselves. We would get up, get dressed in our Sunday best, and Mom would give us each a nickel and five pennies so when the collection plate came around twice, we would have money to put in. Needless to say, I was not learning about tithing. We were not allowed anything to eat before church and receiving the communion wafer. I still to this day do not understand why. I would sit here with a growling tummy waiting for service to be over.

I remember going up for communion one day and coming back to sit down. I noticed some folks were not going up, so I asked the "grown-up" next to me why and they replied, "Oh, that person is divorced," or something to that effect. I have searched the scriptures and I don't see anywhere where Jesus is at the last supper and instructing the apostles to receive the host, but with the following exclusions. I am not condemning anyone here, but this was my experience.

My point here is I was told that God is everywhere, so I figured that if He is everywhere then I don't need to go to church. WRONG, BIG FAT WRONG! Sorry for shouting this out, but I have learned that to be wrong. See, you need to go to church to grow your faith, to hear, to learn, to apply what you have heard and learned to your own life, so we can have life more abundant.

...not forsaking our meeting together [as believers for worship and instruction], as is the habit of some, but encouraging one another; and all the more [faithfully] as you see the day [of Christ's return] approaching.

Hebrews 10:25 (AMP)

The first time I attended a spirit-led church I was extremely apprehensive. I walked in the door and I was hugged by the greeter at the door. I kind of cringed not knowing why this was happening. She was a very nice lady but I just felt uncomfortable.

I was used to growing up attending church and not being allowed to hug the clergy. Many years later, I would get the privilege to be that lady at the door greeting someone else who could really use a welcome with either a handshake, high-five, smile, or maybe even a hug.

I have since then ministered out of a soup kitchen at a Catholic parish and have come to call a certain priest my friend. We have prayed together, and he is very approachable. This was not my experience growing up.

What happens when you visit home? Don't your relatives give you a hug or maybe a smile? Well, church should be the same: a place you consider home and especially a place you feel loved. Regardless of the rubbish going on in your life, all the more reason to be surrounded by a body of believers, your brothers and sisters in Christ who are going to lift you up in prayer and love you through it, not agree with it.

Somebody once asked me, "How do you know it's faith and not mental illness?" "That's a great question I told her. Mental illness will never give you the peace you receive by faith in Christ Jesus."

Peace I leave with you; My [perfect] peace I give to you; not as the world gives do I give to you. Do not let your heart be troubled, nor let it be afraid. [Let My perfect peace calm you in every circumstance and give you courage and strength for every challenge.]

John 14:27 (AMP)

I used to let men and women in my life influence me when it came to having peace in my life. We are the church. We are Christ's ambassadors here on this earth. As such, we should be His example in our everyday interactions with others to bring them closer to Him and not push them away.

Nothing has or will ever come close to the peace that I receive from God. I encourage you to attend a church that is speaking and teaching the gospel of Christ so that you may grow your faith and never allow anyone to keep you from doing so.

As I have been on this journey of growing my faith and learning more about the lover of my soul, I came in contact and fellowship with a very dear, sweet lady who had such a deep religion hurt that it took her to places that tormented her throughout her life spiritually as well as physically. This beautiful lady has fasted and prayed and shares openly her journey of healing.

I pray in the pages following you feel blessed and receive healing from what she has experienced. I love you more, sis.

Religion Hurt Me Too

Christians are expected to live, walk, talk, dress, and act a certain way. When those expectations are not met, we become wounded, broken, and even devastated. I was devastated by people who said they were Christians but did not live up to how I thought Christians should live.

Growing up in a "Christian" home was one of my deepest wounds from Christians. In public, they were Super Christians. You know, spoke all the right words, quoted the Bible like no one's business, acted all spiritual, knew everything about everything, acted all righteous, and dressed the part very well. Behind closed doors at home was a different story. Physical, emotional, sexual, and spiritual abuse was all too common in my home. Being hurt by the people that were supposed to protect and love you began my life of anger, hate, and destruction towards Christians. I didn't see my home as loving, nor did I see my family as Christians.

As a child, I was told that I was going to hell. I didn't know the voice of God and the dreams and visions I would have was a result of my over-active imagination. I learned to never speak unless spoken to, children were only seen and never heard. I didn't belong and wasn't wanted; I was a mistake. Believe me when I say that I came from a so-called Christian home.

In that Christian home I was physically, emotionally, sexually, and spiritually abused. Through all the brokenness and wounding of this, I truly believe God has always had His hand in, on, and over my life. I would talk to Jesus all the time as a kid and I knew that He was talking back to me. I used to run to mother and tell her what Jesus had said to me that day and I would be called a liar and be punished because lying about what Jesus said was a sin and that was a sure way of going to hell. Jesus doesn't talk to children. I really thought that maybe I was crazy. Only crazy people heard voices. I eventually over time started tuning out the voice that I grew accustomed to hearing every day. Praying was a thing of the past for me.

My family members were traveling ministers. We went from church to church ministering and singing. I knew we weren't supposed to be doing this, but who was I to say as much. I knew that what my family was doing was wrong. I became angrier and rebellious.

Pastors would notice that I was unhappy, angry, and miserable. Members of the family would say yeah, we all know she doesn't want to be here, and she is making everyone around her miserable.

I would get pulled into an office of many pastors and talked to. I never spoke about what was going on behind closed doors.

I would sit there and listen to how rebellious children would go to hell; what the family was doing was of God and they didn't need a rebellious kid messing it up for them; I needed to get on board with my family and start acting like a child of God instead of a child of the devil.

The one and only time that I told a pastor what really went on behind closed doors was one of the biggest mistakes of my life. I wasn't able to sit for two weeks and wasn't allowed out of our bus for three I was beaten so severely. That was the day I had lost all respect for pastors and anyone who had any spiritual authority.

The following weeks of recovery I had a lot of alone time to think and dwell. I wasn't talking to God, not because I was mad at Him, but because what was the point in talking to someone that doesn't talk back to children. I do want to point out here that never at any point in my life as a child or an adult was I ever angry with God or ever blamed God for any of this. However, I was very angry, and I was filling my heart with a lot of hate towards anyone who said they were a Christian. I became quiet and very withdrawn from people. My hate was growing daily.

My teenage years weren't any better; I had become so rebellious that I was told there was no hope for me. I was put in counseling and learned really quickly never to speak of my past again. Everything I said went right back to mother.

Straight up, my past stayed right where it belonged, locked up, buried deep and covered with a ten-ton weight of anger and hate. I went down a very, very dark road. At the age of fourteen, I went into Satanism. I was a perfect candidate for this walk of life. For seven years I made it my mission to hurt every Christian I came across and to destroy every church I entered. My anger and hate grew stronger as I was constantly told I was going to burn in hell. At least they had a reason to tell me I was going to hell.

Seven years later, I came out of Satanism. But the hurt didn't stop, it continued. See, I have found that if you don't fit into a church's mold, then you are not one of them. If you don't change to the way they think, you should change, and at a speed they think you should go otherwise you aren't serious about Jesus or changing.

I have never nor will I ever fit into a cookie-cutter mold. That just isn't who I am. I wasn't a good fit in my family's mold or Satan's mold or the church's mold. I couldn't seem to fit in any mold.

I was again hurt by the people that helped me out of Satanism and I left that ministry and didn't serve anyone but myself.

I was on my own, I wasn't a Christian and I wasn't a Satanist. I was tired of it all. When I came out of the closet that I was a homosexual, my mother I had a nervous breakdown. That caused a whole new world of problems.

It was time for me to move away from everyone. I packed up and moved back east. There I made a conscious decision to leave all of my past out west, never to talk about or deal with it. I refused to talk about my life. Out east was a new beginning for me.

How many of us know that the past will always catch up to us one way or another no matter how hard we run? I tried a couple of churches out east but that proved to be pointless. As soon as I mentioned the word "gay," I was asked to leave. I even tried a Metropolitan Community Church; the church was seriously too gay for me. I had a meeting with the pastor there and she tried to tell me that homosexuality was ok in the Bible. She showed me the scripture and I thought, 'No, you have twisted those Scriptures and I will not be coming back.' One thing you don't ever want to do is make Scripture say something other than what it is truly saying. That was the last time I stepped into a church for many years.

The best part of my life starts in this section. I was and continue to this day to receive healing in many areas of my life. I had an obnoxious co-worker convince me to go to a church that she was attending. That was a week of irritation.

I asked what kind of church she went to and she said, "An awesome church." They spoke some funny language and danced and clapped their hands. I was definitely not interested in going. She persisted, and I told my partner that I may be going to church Sunday, but I highly doubted I would go.

The first time I spoke to God in years and this is what I said to Him, "If I get up in time to go to church, I will go." I knew that I wouldn't get up on time to go. I was a night owl. Lo and behold, I was up at 5 am and wide awake. I stayed true to my word and went. When I walked into this church, there was a familiar presence in the house, a presence I hadn't felt in many, many years.

That day was the beginning of the rest of my life. I went through that whole service in awe and amazement. When I returned that night again, I was in utter amazement. I left that night doing a lot of thinking.

I stopped at the store to get a drink and while in the store, I thought what the hell: I went back to the church and the pastor met me halfway down the aisle to ask if he could help me.

I said, "Even if I repent and never have another relationship with another woman, I am still gay. Are you going to kick me out of your church?" He said, "No! Your sin is no different than anyone else's sin. I am just going to love you." Well, I don't know why then, but I took what he said, hook, line, and sinker. My healing began that night.

There were some major issues I had to overcome, but I heard this pastor say one time that it was a season of acceleration. It didn't matter if you were a newborn babe or a fifty-year-old mature Christian. God was doing a healing at an accelerated pace. Now, I don't know about you, but for me, that opened a whole new world to me. To me that meant no matter what issue I had to deal with that it didn't have to take years of therapy or years of struggling, all I had to do is be willing to turn it over to the Lord and He would heal whatever issue came up.

To this day, I still have issues that arise from my past, but I know that with Jesus all I have to do is give it to Him, repent, and forgive others as well as myself.

As time went on and as I sat under this pastor, I was set free of homosexuality. I forgave people that I never thought I would be able to forgive, and I grew very close to Jesus again.

Now, did I get "religion hurt" at this church? Absolutely! See, we pray that God exposes the darkness and the hidden issues in our life that needs to be healed and I don't think people realize that Jesus will answer those prayers. See, my greatest issue for me was "religion hurt." Did God hurt me? No, people did, and believe me it was from a person that I greatly respected. I was accused of a lot of things that day and my heart was shattered into a million pieces. There were a lot of false accusations and there is no greater hurt than a person of God that you greatly respect shredding you to pieces. I was angry, ok, I was furious. I didn't want to go back to that church. I didn't want to see that person ever again.

In my mind, my past of "religion hurt" had caught up with me and I literally wanted to run. I didn't want to face that part of my life. This was the reason I hated Christians; this was the reason I hated spiritual authority; this was the reason I hated church. I had grown to love and respect the people in this church in a very unusually short amount of time.

A friend said to me during this time, "You need to pray and give it over to God. You can only be offended if you allow yourself to be." I knew she was right, but I was furious, and you bet your sweetness I allowed myself to be offended. She was compassionate and hugged me while I cried heartbroken. I went to church because my friend insisted that I go.

I'm the type of person that if you speak truth to me with love and I know it's true, I will hear and obey. Let me tell you, the next four weeks were the hardest weeks of my life.

I would literally sit behind this person and just imagine blowing their head off. I'm being real here. There are many of you that think as I think, or worse. Let me tell you what happened. I had to give all this hurt over to the Lord. I had to forgive this person as well as myself to move forward. It took a lot of prayer on my part and someone praying with me to get to that point. I did not leave that church; I chose to stay and work through it. Because of my willingness to pray and work through this, I was blessed with so much more healing in my life.

Will I get hurt again from the body of Christ? Absolutely! However, I have the keys to work through the hurt. Why will I be hurt again? I choose not to close myself off to the body of Christ. I choose to walk in love. I can only be offended if I allow myself to be. I understand now that there are all kinds of wounded and broken people walking in churches today.

Understanding that people are human, pastors are human, spiritual leaders are human and have their own wounds and hurts to deal with make it a lot easier to deal with religion hurt.

In writing this I have received more healing in my life. I didn't know why I doubted myself so much in the spiritual realm. Remember the ten-ton weight of anger and hate that buried the hurts of my family and pastors? Well, Jesus began peeling back the layers of my past and helping me understand why.

I have always heard and known Scripture says, "My sheep know my voice." Never ask Jesus to reveal the hidden if you're not serious about walking through the healing process.

Deep healing has taken place over my past and I have allowed Jesus Christ to remove the many layers of pain, wounds, brokenness, and put my shattered heart of the past back together.

I have found the real me through this journey. I have found the tender, loving, caring, and compassionate me. You see, Jesus sent me to the right church to begin my healing process.

I gave my all to the Lord, the good, the bad, and the ugly. I have not regretted it for one moment. I have much more healing to go through and I am ready for whatever the Lord shines that light on next. I have never experienced the peace and love of Jesus Christ as I have over the last three years.

We must be willing to allow the Lord to heal those deep and painful wounds in our life. I heard truth and I acted on truth.

The greatest time in my life is now, serving the Master of my life. I continue to move forward and witness for my Jesus and tell people what He has done for me. That ten-ton weight of anger and hate—gone. Praise God!!

I am now back west where Jesus has done major healing between my family and me. It's a continuous process, but I know that Jesus will continue to heal every area of my life as long as I am willing and obedient to Him. Pastors whom I have hurt, we now come together and talk; healing and forgiveness is taking place. When we are in God's timing and are obedient to Him, all things work out for the Glory of God. No matter how bad we have been hurt or have hurt others the one thing I know deep in my spirit is that Jesus is in the restoration business.

Love ya more,

Sis

Walls—It Might Just Take a Team

Have you ever heard it takes a village to raise a child? Well, I believe in our spiritual walk it takes a team to peel away the layers of our spiritual wrong guidance and help to guide us in our spirit-led maturing.

Sometimes it takes a team to break down those walls. After all, it may have taken a team to help put them up. Past hurts, abuse, the list can be endless. Some folks receive their healing right away. It took a team for my healing. I am speaking from my own experience.

We are aware of the five-fold ministry, yes five, not four: pastors, teachers, evangelists, prophets, and apostles. Each carrying its own mantle.

Apostle - messenger of God.

Prophet - prophesy into your life and offer correction.

Teacher – teach you the Word.

Pastor – responsible for helping you grow your faith.

Evangelist – publicly speaks the Word of God for redemption.

Now, these are just a short definition of what these anointed mantles carry without going into their full definitions. They are all guided by the Holy Spirit.

In life, it was like I was in a desolate land, no trees, no people, just dust everywhere. I was a hot mess.

It took a divine team equipped with the Spirit of God to heal my spirit. When my spirit healed, I began recognizing just how many times God tried to reach out to me. Each time I would just push Him away because it was uncomfortable with my flesh.

I had to take control of my flesh. I had to repent and when I did, I noticed such a change that I did not recognize the person I was before Christ. When I met other people and shared my testimony, they could not believe that was who I used to be.

> *Therefore if anyone is in Christ [that is, grafted in, joined to Him by faith in Him as Savior], he is a new creature [reborn and renewed by the Holy Spirit]; the old things [the previous moral and spiritual condition] have passed away. Behold, new things have come [because spiritual awakening brings a new life].*
>
> 2 Corinthians 5:17 (AMP)

And [His gifts to the church were varied and] He Himself appointed some as apostles [special messengers, representatives], some as prophets [who speak a new message from God to the people], some as evangelists [who spread the good news of salvation], and some as pastors and teachers [to shepherd and guide and instruct], [and He did this] to fully equip and perfect the saints (God's people) for works of service, to build up the body of Christ [the church]; until we all reach oneness in the faith and in the knowledge of the Son of God, [growing spiritually] to become a mature believer, reaching to the measure of the fullness of Christ [manifesting His spiritual completeness and exercising our spiritual gifts in unity]. So that we are no longer children [spiritually immature], tossed back and forth [like ships on a stormy sea] and carried about by every wind of [shifting] doctrine, by the cunning and trickery of [unscrupulous] men, by the deceitful scheming of people ready to do anything [for personal profit]. But speaking the truth in love [in all things—both our speech and our lives expressing His truth], let us grow up in all things into Him [following His example] who is the Head—Christ. From Him the whole body [the church, in all its various parts], joined and knitted firmly together by what every joint supplies, when *each part is working properly, causes the body to grow and mature, building itself up [a]in [unselfish] love.*

Ephesians 4:11-16 (AMP)

Until I opened my heart to receive what these anointed individuals carried in their giftings, I suffered not knowing who I truly was. It was almost a tag-team effort. The layers of religion and wrong teachings began to peel away revealing the spirit of God within.

Now the Lord is the Spirit, and where the Spirit of the Lord is, there is liberty [emancipation from bondage, true freedom].

2 Corinthians 3:17 (AMP)

Comforter - counselor, helper, intercessor, advocate, strengthener, standby, Holy Spirit

God is the ultimate comforter and brings peace and comfort during all storms. He sent the Holy Spirit to be our Comforter.

But I tell you the truth, it is to your advantage that I go away; for if I do not go away, the Helper (Comforter, Advocate, Intercessor—Counselor, Strengthener, Standby) will not come to you; but if I go, I will send Him (the Holy Spirit) to you [to be in close fellowship with you].

John 16:7 (AMP)

I pray that you search the Word of God for your answer to life's questions and allow the Holy Spirit to comfort and help you.

In some cases, so many walls are up because of strongholds (belief systems), past hurts, personal prisons that a team effort is required for a total breakout. Not breakthrough.

I pray that you have an open heart to receive what the Word of God has prepared for you and that your spirit will hunger and thirst for the things of God and His righteousness.

In Closing

When we come to the realization of who we are as His children on this earth then, and only then, will we stop settling for less than we deserve. One person can stand and make a difference.

Many faithful children united will change the world. Now don't go burning your bra just yet, that is not what I am talking about. I am talking about being loving enough to reach out to others in need and share the love of Christ with them, to let them know they are not alone. Strong enough to share how God has strengthened us and share your testimonies. Radical enough to know that those testimonies are now tools that God is using to minister to those in need. These tools are not there to remind you of a darker time. They can no longer harm you or accuse you.

I long for the day when domestic violence, and sexual assault among other sufferings are a thing of the past where the next generation has to search for information on these subjects in Wikipedia, because they have no point of reference. No one should ever suffer at the hands of an abuser the violence must stop. We are too valuable. We are His children and we are loved.

- Every nine seconds in the U.S. a woman is assaulted or beaten.
- Around the world, at least one in every three women has been beaten, coerced into sex, or otherwise abused during her lifetime. Most often, the abuser is a member of her own family.
- Domestic violence is the leading cause of injury to women – more than car accidents, muggings, and rapes combined.
- Studies suggest that up to ten million children witness some form of domestic violence annually.
- Nearly one in five teenage girls who have been in a relationship said a boyfriend threatened violence or self-harm if presented with a breakup.
- Every day in the U.S. more than three women are murdered by their husbands or boyfriends.
- Ninety-two percent of women surveyed listed reducing domestic violence and sexual assault as their top concern.
- Domestic violence victims lose nearly eight million days of paid work per year in the U.S. alone – the equivalent of 32,000 full-time jobs.

- Based on reports from ten countries, between 55% and 95% of women who had been physically abused by their parents had never contacted non-governmental organizations, shelters, or the police for help.
- The costs of intimate partner violence in the U.S. alone exceed $5.8 billion per year. $4.1 billion are for direct medical and health care services, while productivity losses account for nearly $1.8 billion.
- Men who as children witnessed their parents' domestic violence were twice as likely to abuse their own wives than sons of nonviolent parents.
- These statistics are dated as of June of 2020
- via *domesticviolencestatistics.org* website.

I do not pray for these alone [it is not for their sake only that I make this request], but also for [all] those who [will ever] believe and trust in Me through their message, that they all may be one; just as You, Father, are in Me and I in You, that they also may be one in Us, so that the world may believe [without any doubt] that You sent Me. I have given to them the glory and honor which You have given Me, that they may be one, just as We are one; I in them and You in Me, that they may be perfected and completed into one, so that the world

may know [without any doubt] that You sent Me,
and [that You] have loved them, just as You have
loved Me.

John 17:20-23 (AMP)

He gives strength to the weary, and to him who
has no might He increases power. Even youths
grow weary and tired, And vigorous young men
stumble badly, But those who wait for the Lord
[who expect, look for, and hope in Him] Will gain
new strength and renew their power; They will lift
up their wings [and rise up close to God] like eagles
[rising toward the sun]; They will run and not be-
come weary, They will walk and not grow tired.

Isaiah 40:29-31 (AMP)

They looked to Him and were radiant;
Their faces will never blush in shame or confusion.

Psalm 34:5 (AMP)

Now the Lord is the Spirit, and where the Spirit of the Lord
is, there is liberty [emancipation from bondage, true freedom].

2 Corinthians 3:17 (AMP)

National Hotlines

www.211.org or call 211 on your phone covers:
*Crisis and emergency
*Disaster assistance
*Food
*Health
*Housing and Utilities
*Human trafficking
*Jobs and support
*Re-entry
*Veterans

National Resource Center on Domestic Violence
1-800-537-2238

National Domestic Violence Hotline 1-800-799-7233

Legal Help

Womenslaw.org   They only give help via the email. Regardless of gender, call the National Domestic Violence Hotline for help over the phone at 800-799-7233.

National Suicide Prevention Lifeline 800-273-8255

Crisisnetwork.org

Online support for loss of a child *https://www.compassionatefriends.org*

Samaritans Hotline 24 Hour Emotional support 212-673-3000

Veteransline.net 1-800-273-8255

Americanaddictioncenters.org 888-638-1803

Contact the Author

To contact the author, Lisa Adams, her website and email address are:

https://onefiercelady.wixsite.com/fierce
onefiercelady@outlook.com

Journaling Notes

_____

_____

_____

_____

_____

_____

_____

_____

_____

_____

_____

_____

_____

_____

_____

_____

_____

_____

_____

_____